easy to make!
Slow Cook

Good Housekeeping

easy to make!
Slow Cook

COLLINS & BROWN

This edition published in the United Kingdom in 2015
by Collins & Brown
1 Gower Street
London WC1E 6HD

An imprint of Pavilion Books Company Ltd

The Good Housekeeping website is
www.goodhousekeeping.co.uk

10 9 8 7 6 5 4 3

ISBN 978-1-84340-651-8

A catalogue record for this book is available from the British
Library.

Reproduction by Dot Gradations UK, Ltd
Printed and bound by Times Offset (M) Sdn. Bhd, Malaysia

This book can be ordered direct from the publisher at
www.pavilionbooks.com

Contents

Foreword

Cooking, for me, is one of life's great pleasures. Not only is it necessary to fuel your body, but it exercises creativity, skill, social bonding and patience. The science behind the cooking also fascinates me, learning to understand how yeast works, or to grasp why certain flavours marry quite so well (in my mind) is to become a good cook.

I've often encountered people who claim not to be able to cook – they're just not interested or say they simply don't have time. My sister won't mind me saying that she was one of those who sat firmly in the camp of disinterested domestic goddess. But things change, she realised that my mother (an excellent cook) can't always be on hand to prepare steaming home-cooked meals and that she actually wanted to become a mother one day who was able to whip up good food for her own family. All it took was some good cook books (naturally, Good Housekeeping was present and accounted for) and some enthusiasm and sure enough she is now a kitchen wizard, creating such confections that even baffle me.

I've been lucky enough to have had a love for all things culinary since as long as I can remember. Baking rock-like chocolate cakes and misshapen biscuits was a right of passage that I protectively guard. I made my mistakes young, so have lost the fear of cookery mishaps. I think it's these mishaps that scare people, but when you realise that a mistake made once will seldom be repeated, then kitchen domination can start.

This Good Housekeeping Easy to Make! collection is filled with hundreds of tantalising recipes that have been triple tested (at least!) in our dedicated test kitchens. They have been developed to be easily achievable, delicious and guaranteed to work – taking the chance out of cooking.

I hope you enjoy this collection and that it inspires you to get cooking.

Meike.

Meike Beck
Cookery Editor
Good Housekeeping

0

The Basics

Making stock
Preparing and cooking meat
Preparing and cooking poultry
Preparing vegetables
Cooking vegetables
Preparing and cooking fruit
Using a slow cooker
Food storage and hygiene

Making stock

Good stock can make the difference between a good soup and a great one. It also gives depth of flavour to many dishes. There are four main types of stock: vegetable, meat, chicken and fish.

Cook's Tips

- To get a clearer liquid when making fish, meat or poultry stock, strain the cooked stock through four layers of muslin in a sieve.
- Stock will keep for three days in the refrigerator. If you want to keep it for a further three days, transfer it to a pan and reboil gently for five minutes. Cool, put in a clean bowl and chill for a further three days.
- When making meat or poultry stock, make sure there is a good ratio of meat to bones. The more meat you use, the more flavour the stock will have.

Stocks

Vegetable Stock

For 1.2 litres (2 pints), you will need:
225g (8oz) each onions, celery, leeks and carrots, chopped, 1 bouquet garni (2 bay leaves, a few thyme sprigs, 1 small bunch of parsley), 10 black peppercorns, ½ tsp salt.

1 Put all the ingredients into a large pan and add 1.7 litres (3 pints) cold water. Bring slowly to the boil and skim the surface.

2 Partially cover the pan and simmer for 30 minutes. Adjust the seasoning if necessary. Strain the stock through a fine sieve into a bowl and leave to cool.

Meat Stock

For 900ml (1½ pints), you will need:
450g (1lb) each meat bones and stewing meat, 1 onion, 2 celery sticks and 1 large carrot, sliced, 1 bouquet garni (2 bay leaves, a few thyme sprigs, 1 small bunch of parsley), 1 tsp black peppercorns, ½ tsp salt.

1 Preheat the oven to 220°C (200°C fan oven) mark 7. Put the meat and bones into a roasting tin and roast for 30–40 minutes, turning now and again, until they are well browned.

2 Put the bones into a large pan with the remaining ingredients and add 2 litres (3½ pints) cold water. Bring slowly to the boil and skim the surface.

3 Partially cover the pan and simmer for 4–5 hours. Adjust the seasoning if necessary. Strain through a muslin-lined sieve into a bowl and cool quickly. Degrease (see opposite) before using.

Chicken Stock

For 1.2 litres (2 pints), you will need:
1.6kg (3½lb) chicken bones, 225g (8oz) each onions
and celery, sliced, 150g (5oz) chopped leeks,
1 bouquet garni (2 bay leaves, a few thyme sprigs,
1 small bunch of parsley), 1 tsp black peppercorns,
½ tsp salt.

1 Put all the ingredients into a large pan and add 3
litres (5¼ pints) cold water. Bring slowly to the
boil and skim the surface.

2 Partially cover the pan and simmer gently for 2
hours. Adjust the seasoning if necessary.

3 Strain the stock through a muslin-lined sieve into
a bowl and cool quickly. Degrease (see right)
before using.

Fish Stock

For 900ml (1½ pints), you will need:
900g (2lb) fish bones and trimmings, washed,
2 carrots, 1 onion and 2 celery sticks, sliced,
1 bouquet garni (2 bay leaves, a few thyme sprigs,
1 small bunch of parsley), 6 white peppercorns,
½ tsp salt.

1 Put all the ingredients into a large pan and add
900ml (1½ pints) cold water. Bring slowly to the
boil and skim the surface.

2 Partially cover the pan and simmer gently for
30 minutes. Adjust the seasoning if necessary.

3 Strain through a muslin-lined sieve into a bowl
and cool quickly. Fish stock tends not to have
much fat in it and so does not usually need to
be degreased. However, if it does seem to be fatty,
you will need to remove this by degreasing it
(see right).

Degreasing stock

Meat and poultry stock needs to be degreased. (Vegetable
stock does not.) You can mop the fat from the surface
using kitchen paper, but the following methods are easier
and more effective. There are three main methods that
you can use: ladling, pouring and chilling.

1 **Ladling** While the stock is warm, place a ladle on
the surface. Press down and allow the fat floating on
the surface to trickle over the edge until the ladle is
full. Discard the fat, then repeat until all the fat has
been removed.

2 **Pouring** For this you need a degreasing jug or a
double-pouring gravy boat, which has the spout
at the base of the vessel. When you fill the jug or
gravy boat with a fatty liquid, the fat rises. When
you pour, the stock comes out while the fat stays
behind in the jug.

3 **Chilling** This technique works best with stock made
from meat, as the fat solidifies when cold. Put the
stock in the refrigerator until the fat becomes solid,
then remove the pieces of fat using a slotted spoon.

Preparing and cooking meat

Beef, lamb, pork, ham and game such as rabbit and venison make wonderfully hearty one-pot meals, and are easy to prepare and cook when you know how. For perfectly cooked meat, choose the appropriate method for the cut. Tender cuts need quick cooking, such as grilling, whereas tougher cuts benefit from slower cooking, such as pot-roasting.

Trimming meat

Trim away excess fat, leaving no more than 5mm (¼in) on steaks, chops and roasting cuts – a little fat will contribute juiciness and flavour. When preparing meat for cutting into chunks, try to separate the individual muscles, which can be identified by the sinews running between each muscle.

Marinades

Meat is good for marinating, either wet or dry, because its large surface area allows maximum exposure to the marinade. Marinate small pieces of meat for at least 8 hours, and thick joints for 24 hours.

Wet marinades

These almost always contain some form of acid, which has a modest tenderising effect (especially in thin cuts such as steak). Before cooking, dry marinated meat thoroughly to remove liquid from the surface, and cook the marinade (skimming off the oil if necessary) as a sauce or deglazing liquid.

Good additions to wet marinades:
• Onions and shallots, chopped or sliced
• Asian spices, such as Chinese five-spice powder and star anise
• Chilli
• Sherry or sherry vinegar
• Brandy

Dry marinades

These are useful for roasts and pot roasts. They don't penetrate far into the meat, but give an excellent flavour on and just under the crust. Make them with crushed garlic, dried herbs or spices, and plenty of freshly ground black pepper. Rub into the meat and marinate for at least 30 minutes or up to 8 hours.

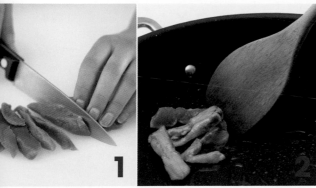

Stir-frying

Perfect for tender cuts of meat.

1 Trim the fat, then cut the meat into strips or dice no thicker than 5mm (¹/₄in).

2 Heat a wok or large pan until hot and add oil to coat the inside. Add the meat and cook, stirring. Set aside. Cook the other ingredients you are using (such as vegetables and flavourings). Return the meat to the wok for 1–2 minutes to heat through.

Braising and pot-roasting

Tougher cuts of meat (see bottom of page) require slow cooking. Braises and pot roasts are similar, but braises need more liquid.

To serve 6, you will need:
3 tbsp olive oil, 1.1kg (2¹/₂lb) meat, cut into large chunks, or 6 lamb shanks, 1 large onion, 3 carrots, 3 celery sticks, all thickly sliced, 2 garlic cloves, crushed, 2 x 400g cans chopped tomatoes, 150ml (¹/₄ pint) white wine, salt and ground black pepper, 2 bay leaves.

1 Preheat the oven to 170°C (150°C fan oven) mark 3. Heat the oil in a large flameproof casserole and lightly brown the meat all over, in two or three batches. Remove from the pan; set aside. Add the onion, carrots, celery and garlic and cook until beginning to colour, then add the meat, tomatoes and wine.

2 Stir well, season and add the bay leaves. Bring to the boil, cover, and transfer to the oven for 2 hours or until tender. Skim off fat if necessary.

Perfect braising and pot-roasting

- Good cuts of beef include shin, chuck, blade, brisket and flank; good cuts of lamb include leg, shoulder, neck, breast and shank; good cuts of pork include shoulder, hand, spring, belly and loin.
- Cuts you would normally roast can also be casseroled. These simply need less time in the oven.
- Always use a low heat, and check regularly to make sure that there is enough liquid to keep the meat from catching on the casserole.
- Braises often improve by being cooked in advance and then gently reheated before serving. If you've braised a whole piece of meat, you can slice it before reheating.

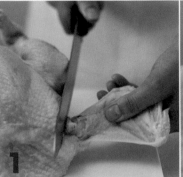

Preparing and cooking poultry

From the simplest, healthiest stir-frying, steaming and poaching to the more robust pot-roasting and casseroling, there are numerous ways to make the most of the delicate taste of poultry.

Jointing

You can buy pieces of chicken in a supermarket or from a butcher, but it is more economical to joint a whole bird yourself. Use the wing tips and bones to make stock (see page 11).

1 Using a sharp meat knife with a curved blade, cut out the wishbone and remove the wings in a single piece. Remove the wing tips.

2 With the tail pointing towards you and breast side up, pull one leg away and cut through the skin between leg and breast. Pull the leg down until you crack the joint between the thigh bone and ribcage. Cut through that joint, then cut through the remaining leg meat. Repeat on the other side.

3 To remove the breast without any bone, make a cut along the length of the breastbone. Gently teasing the flesh away from the ribs with the knife, work the blade down between the flesh and ribs of one breast and cut it off neatly. (Always cut in, towards the bone.) Repeat on the other side.

4 To remove the breast with the bone in, make a cut along the full length of the breastbone. Using poultry shears, cut through the breastbone, then cut through the ribcage following the outline of the breast meat. Repeat on the other side. Trim off any flaps of skin or fat.

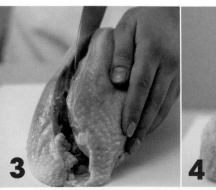

Pot-roasting

To serve 4–6, you will need:
2 tbsp vegetable oil, 1 onion, cut into wedges, 2 rashers rindless streaky bacon, chopped, 1.4–1.6kg (3–3½lb) chicken, 2 small turnips, cut into wedges, 6 carrots, halved, 1 garlic clove, crushed, bouquet garni (see page 127), 600ml (1 pint) chicken stock, 100ml (3½fl oz) dry white wine, small handful of parsley, chopped, salt and pepper.

1 Preheat the oven to 200°C (180°C fan oven) mark 6. Heat the oil in a flameproof casserole. Fry the onion and bacon for 5 minutes. Set aside. Add the chicken, brown all over for 10 minutes, then set aside. Fry the turnips, carrots and garlic for 2 minutes, then add the bacon, onion and chicken.

2 Add the bouquet garni, stock, wine and season. Bring to the boil and transfer to the oven. Cook, basting now and then, for 1 hour 20 minutes or until the juices run clear. Lift out the chicken, stir parsley into the liquid and carve the chicken.

Casseroling

To serve 4–6, you will need:
1 chicken, jointed, 3 tbsp oil, 1 onion, chopped, 2 garlic cloves, crushed, 2 celery sticks, chopped, 2 carrots, chopped, 1 tbsp plain flour, 2 tbsp chopped tarragon or thyme, chicken stock and/or wine, salt and pepper.

1 Preheat the oven to 180°C (160°C fan oven) mark 4. Cut the chicken legs and breasts in half.

2 Heat the oil in a flameproof casserole and brown the chicken all over. Remove and pour off the excess oil. Add the onion and garlic and brown for a few minutes. Add the vegetables, then stir in the flour and cook for 1 minute. Add the herbs and season. Add the chicken and pour in stock and/or wine to come three-quarters of the way up the poultry. Cook for 1–1½ hours.

Poaching

This gentle method of cooking will produce a light broth.

1 Brown the bird in oil if you like (this is not necessary but will give a deeper flavour), then transfer to a pan that will hold it easily: a large frying pan or sauté pan is good for pieces, a flameproof casserole for a whole bird.

2 Add 1 roughly chopped onion, 2 crushed garlic cloves, 2 chopped carrots, 2 chopped celery sticks, 6 whole black peppercorns and 1 tsp dried mixed herbs. Pour in just enough stock to cover, then simmer, uncovered, for 30–40 minutes (for pieces) or about 1 hour (for a whole bird).

3 Gently lift the bird out of the liquid. If you are planning to use the liquid as the basis for a sauce, reduce it by at least half.

Perfect pot-roasted poultry

- Pot-roasting is the perfect way to cook almost any poultry or game bird apart from duck or goose, which are too fatty and do not give good results, and turkey, which is too large to fit in the average casserole dish.
- Make sure that you use a large enough casserole and that the bird isn't too close to the sides of the dish.
- Check the liquid level in the casserole from time to time. If it's too dry, add a little more. Water is fine; stock or wine is even better.
- Timings for pot-roasted poultry: about 45 minutes (for small birds such as poussin) or 1–1½ hours (for chicken or guinea fowl).

2

3

4

Preparing vegetables

The following frequently used vegetables can be quickly prepared to add flavour to savoury dishes. Onions and shallots have a pungent taste that becomes milder when they are cooked, and they are often used as a basic flavouring. Tomatoes and peppers add depth and richness to a variety of dishes. Garlic and chillies are stronger flavouring ingredients.

Onions

1 Cut off the tip and base of the onion. Peel away all the layers of papery skin and any discoloured layers underneath.

2 Put the onion, root end down, on the chopping board, then, using a sharp knife, cut the onion in half from tip to base.

3 **Slicing** Put one half on the board, with the cut surface facing down, and slice across the onion.

4 **Chopping** Slice the halved onions from the root end to the top at regular intervals. Next, make two or three horizontal slices through the onion, then slice vertically across the width.

Seeding peppers

1 Cut the pepper in half vertically and snap out the white pithy core and seeds. Trim away the rest of the white membrane with a knife.

2 Alternatively, slice off the top of the pepper, then cut away and discard the seeds and white pith.

Garlic

1 Put the clove on a chopping board and place the flat side of a large knife on top of it. Press down firmly on the flat of the blade to crush the clove and break the papery skin.

2 Cut off the base of the clove and slip the garlic out of its skin.

3 **Slicing** Using a rocking motion with the knife tip on the board, slice the garlic as thinly as you need.

4 **Shredding and chopping** Holding the slices together, shred them across the slices. Chop the shreds if you need chopped garlic.

5 **Crushing** After step 2, either use a garlic press or crush with a knife: roughly chop the peeled cloves and put them on the board with a pinch of salt. Press down hard with the edge of a large knife tip (with the blade facing away from you), then drag the blade along the garlic while still pressing hard. Continue to do this, dragging the knife tip over the garlic to make a purée.

Seeding unpeeled tomatoes

1 Halve the tomato through the core. Use a small sharp knife or a spoon to remove the seeds and juice. Shake off the excess liquid.

2 Chop the tomato as required for the recipe and place in a colander for a minute or two to drain off any excess liquid.

Chillies

1 Cut off the cap and slit open lengthways. Using a spoon, scrape out the seeds and the pith.

2 For diced chilli, cut into thin shreds lengthways, then cut crossways.

Cook's Tip

Wash hands thoroughly after handling chillies – the volatile oils will sting if accidentally rubbed into your eyes.

Cooking vegetables

Nutritious, mouthwatering and essential to a healthy diet – vegetables are ideal for adding to one-pot dishes.

Stir-frying

Stir-frying is perfect for non-starchy vegetables, as the quick cooking preserves their colour, freshness and texture.

To serve 4, you will need:
450g (1lb) vegetables, 1–2 tbsp vegetable oil, 2 garlic cloves, crushed, 2 tbsp soy sauce, 2 tsp sesame oil.

1 Cut the vegetables into even-sized pieces. Heat the oil in a large wok or frying pan until smoking-hot. Add the garlic and cook for a few seconds, then remove and set aside.

2 Add the vegetables to the wok, and toss and stir them. Keep them moving constantly as they cook, which will take 4–5 minutes.

3 When the vegetables are just tender, but still with a slight bite, turn off the heat. Put the garlic back into the wok and stir well. Add the soy sauce and sesame oil, toss and serve.

Perfect stir-frying

- Cut everything into small pieces of uniform size so that they cook quickly and evenly.
- If you're cooking onions or garlic with the vegetables, don't keep them over a high heat for too long or they will burn.
- Add liquids towards the end of cooking, so they don't evaporate.

Stewing

1 Cut the vegetables into large, bite-sized pieces, no more than about 5cm (2in) square. Put them into a heatproof casserole (for oven cooking) or a heavy-based pan (for hob cooking). Add salt and pepper and flavourings if you like (see Perfect stews below), and mix well.

2 Preheat the oven to 180°C (160°C fan oven) mark 4 if you are cooking in the oven.

3 Pour in stock to come about three-quarters of the way up the vegetables. Cover the dish with a lid or foil and cook for 30–40 minutes until the vegetables are tender but not disintegrating.

4 Turn the vegetables once during cooking, and baste with the juices a few times.

Perfect stews

- Any vegetable can be stewed; be careful not to overcook it.
- Ideal flavourings for stewed vegetables include garlic, shallots, curry powder (or Indian spices), and chilli sauce or chopped chilli.
- Potatoes will thicken the dish a little as they release some of their starch.

Perfect braising

- Carrots, fennel, leeks, celeriac, celery and cabbage are good braised.
- Leave vegetables whole or cut into chunks. Shred cabbage, then fry lightly before braising.
- Cook the vegetables in a single layer.

Braising

1 Prepare the vegetables (see Perfect braising below left). Pack tightly in an ovenproof dish. Preheat the oven to 180°C (160°C fan oven) mark 4. Dot generously with butter and season with salt.

2 Pour in stock to come halfway up the vegetables. Cover and bake for 30–40 minutes until the vegetables are soft. Baste them with the buttery stock a few times during cooking.

3

4

Preparing and cooking fruit

Most fruits taste marvellous raw, although a few always need to be cooked. Nearly all fruits make superb desserts when they are baked, poached or stewed.

Classic Poached Pears

To serve 4, you will need:
300g (11oz) sugar, 4 ripe pears, juice of 1 lemon.

1 Put the sugar in a large measuring jug and fill with cold water to make 1 litre (1³/₄ pints). Transfer to a pan and heat gently, stirring now and then, until the sugar has dissolved.

2 Peel and halve the pears, and toss gently with lemon juice.

3 Pour the sugar syrup into a wide-based pan and bring to a simmer. Put in the pears, cut sides down. They should be completely covered with syrup: add a little more syrup if necessary.

4 Simmer the fruit very gently for 30–40 minutes until the pears are soft when pierced with a knife. Serve hot, warm or cold.

Baking

The key to success when baking fruit is in keeping the cooking time short, so that the delicate flesh of the fruit doesn't break down completely. Preheat the oven to 200°C (180°C fan oven) mark 6.

1 Prepare the fruit and put in a single layer in a greased baking dish or individual dishes. Put a splash of water in the bottom of the dish(es). (For extra flavour, you can use fruit juice or wine instead of water, if you prefer.) Sprinkle with sugar (and other flavourings such as spices, citrus zest or vanilla, if you like). Dot with butter.

2 Bake the fruit until just tender when pierced with a knife or skewer: this should take 15–25 minutes depending on the fruit and the size of the pieces. Leave to rest for a few minutes before serving.

Good fruits for baking

Fruit	Preparation
Apples (dessert or cooking)	Cored and halved or quartered
Apricots	Whole, or halved and stoned
Bananas	Peeled and halved, or in their skins
Berries	Whole
Nectarines and peaches	Halved and stoned
Pears	Cored and halved or quartered
Pineapple	Cored and cut into large chunks
Plums	Whole, or halved and stoned

Stewing

To serve 4, you will need:
450g (1lb) prepared fruit (chunks of apples and rhubarb, whole gooseberries, halved plums), sugar to taste, 1 tbsp lemon juice.

1 Put the fruit in a non-stick stainless-steel pan with the sugar. Add the lemon juice and 2 tbsp water. Bring to the boil over a medium heat, then turn down the heat and simmer gently, partly covered, until the fruit is soft, stirring often.

Zesting citrus fruits

Citrus zest is an important flavouring and is simple to prepare.

1 Wash and thoroughly dry the fruit. Using a vegetable peeler or small sharp knife, cut away the zest (the coloured outer layer of skin), taking care to leave behind the bitter white pith. Continue until you have removed as much as you need.

2 Stack the slices of zest on a board and shred or dice as required using a sharp knife.

Easy zesting

- To use a zester, press the blade into the citrus skin and run it along the surface to take off long shreds.
- To use a grater, rub the fruit over the grater, using a medium pressure to remove the zest without taking off the white pith as well.

What is a slow cooker and how does it work?

A slow cooker is a standalone electrical appliance, designed to be plugged in and left gently cooking unsupervised for hours, without burning or drying up the food. It consists of a lidded round or oval earthenware or ceramic pot that sits in a metal housing containing the heating element, which heats the contents to a steady temperature of around 100°C. Little steam can escape and it condenses in the lid, forming a seal that keeps the temperature constant and the food moist. It also means that a suet pudding can be left to cook for hours without needing to top up the water.

Depending on the model, there are two or three cooking settings (Low, Medium and High) and a Keep Warm function. These settings give you the option to cook a dish on High for just a few hours or on Low all day or overnight. Multi-functional models can also be used as rice cookers and steamers. Older-style slow cookers have a fixed pot to contain the food, but, nowadays, most contain a removable, dishwasher-friendly pot that can be taken straight to the table for serving.

Want to save on washing up? Choose a removable pot that can be used to start off the dish on the hob then transferred to the slow cooker unit. Alternatively, use slow cooker liners (available from specialist websites) if you have a fixed pot cooker.

Using a slow cooker

A slow cooker is perfect for the cook with a busy lifestyle. We relish the stews and casseroles our grandmothers would have dished up for a midweek supper without a second thought, but now they're a treat for the weekend when we have more time to prepare them. However, a slow cooker solves that problem: switch it on as you leave in the morning and you'll return home at the end of the day to a delicious, home-cooked meal.

Choosing a slow cooker

Anyone can use a slow cooker: some models are ideal for large families or the cook who likes to stock up the freezer, while smaller versions are suitable for couples or for students living in a bedsit. Otherwise, choose yours according to what you most like to cook: are you only planning to use it for casseroles, will you want to cook a whole chicken or are you hoping to make plenty of steamed puddings? Make sure you check the size before you buy.

What you can cook in a slow cooker

Practically anything! Don't just stick to soups, stews and casseroles. You can steam suet puddings (a brilliant hob-space saver at Christmas time), braise joints of meat and whole chickens and even bake cakes and make pâtés. Set it to cook overnight and you can enjoy a bowl of warming porridge for breakfast too. Cooking food in a slow cooker has many benefits: flavours have time to develop and even the toughest of cuts of meat become incredibly tender. It's important to raise the temperature quickly to destroy harmful bacteria so, either bring the food to boiling point on the hob first or preheat the slow cooker – always follow the manufacturer's instructions.

What you can't cook in a slow cooker

Not much! But obviously very large joints of meat and poultry such as turkey aren't suitable, while roasts and stir-fries are out of the question. Some foods, such as pasta, rice, fish, puddings and cakes, are only suitable for shorter slow cooking times so always check the recipe. Milk and cream will separate if cooked for a long time – add them to finish off and enrich a dish in the last few minutes or so of cooking time. Always fully immerse potatoes to stop them blackening while cooking.

Saving money with a slow cooker

Not only are slow cookers practical, they're economical, too, because:

- Tougher cuts of meat, such as oxtail, shin of beef or lamb shanks tend to be cheaper and benefit from long, slow cooking at low temperatures. Perfect for the slow cooker.
- It uses far less energy than a conventional oven because you are only heating up a small piece of equipment that runs on a minute amount of power in comparison.
- They're ideal for flexible meal times, saving you cash and conserving energy. It's especially useful for large active families who eat at different times – prepare one dish then keep it warm in the pot for up to two hours.

Slow cooker safety tips

- Always stand the appliance on a heat-resistant surface.
- Do not use a slow cooker to reheat cold or frozen food – the temperature rises too slowly to kill harmful bacteria. Heat first on the hob then transfer to the slow cooker pot.
- Always use oven gloves to remove the pot from the slow cooker.
- Never immerse the outer housing in water; stand on a draining board to clean and remove the flex if possible.
- Never fill the outer housing with food; always use the inner pot.
- Don't let young children touch the slow cooker – the housing and the lid can become hot or spit boiling water.
- Be careful when cooking with dried beans – for example, kidney beans need to be boiled vigorously for 10 minutes to remove harmful toxins. Do this in a pan on the hob before draining and continuing with the recipe in the slow cooker.

Hygiene

When you are preparing food, always follow these important guidelines.

Wash your hands thoroughly before handling food and again between handling different types of food, such as raw and cooked meat and poultry. If you have any cuts or grazes on your hands, be sure to keep them covered with a waterproof plaster.

Wash down worksurfaces regularly with a mild detergent solution or multi-surface cleaner.

Use a dishwasher if available. Otherwise, wear rubber gloves for washing-up, so that the water temperature can be hotter than unprotected hands can bear. Wash and change drying-up cloths and cleaning cloths regularly. Note that leaving dishes to drain is more hygienic than drying them with a teatowel.

Keep pets out of the kitchen if possible; or make sure they stay away from worksurfaces. Never allow animals on to worksurfaces.

Shopping

Always choose fresh ingredients in prime condition from stores and markets that have a regular turnover of stock to ensure you buy the freshest produce possible.

Make sure items are within their 'best before' or 'use by' date. (Foods with a longer shelf life have a 'best before' date; more perishable items have a 'use by' date.)

Pack frozen and chilled items in an insulated cool bag at the check-out and put them into the freezer or refrigerator as soon as you get home.

During warm weather in particular, buy perishable foods just before you return home. When packing items at the check-out, sort them according to where you will store them when you get home – the refrigerator, freezer, storecupboard, vegetable rack, fruit bowl, etc. This will make unpacking easier – and quicker.

Food storage and hygiene

Storing food properly and preparing it in a hygienic way is important to ensure that it remains as nutritious and flavourful as possible, and to reduce the risk of food poisoning.

The storecupboard

Although storecupboard ingredients generally last a long time, correct storage is important.

Always check packaging for storage advice – even with familiar foods, because storage requirements may change if additives, sugar or salt have been reduced. Check storecupboard foods for their 'best before' or 'use by' date and do not use them if the date has passed.

Keep all food cupboards scrupulously clean and make sure food containers and packets are properly sealed.

Once opened, treat canned foods as though fresh. Always transfer the contents to a clean container, cover and keep in the refrigerator. Similarly, jars, sauce bottles and cartons should be kept chilled after opening. (Check the label for storage time after opening.)

Transfer dry goods such as sugar, rice and pasta to moisture-proof containers. When supplies are used up, wash the container well and dry thoroughly before refilling with new supplies.

Store oils in a dark cupboard away from any heat source as heat and light can make them turn rancid and affect their colour. For the same reason, buy olive oil in dark green bottles.

Store vinegars in a cool place; they can turn bad in a warm environment.

Store dried herbs, spices and flavourings in a cool, dark cupboard or in dark jars. Buy in small quantities as their flavour will not last indefinitely.

Store flour and sugar in airtight containers.

Refrigerator storage

Fresh food needs to be kept in the cool temperature of a refrigerator to keep it in good condition and discourage the growth of harmful bacteria. Store day-to-day perishable items, such as opened jams and jellies, mayonnaise and bottled sauces, in the refrigerator along with eggs and dairy products, fruit juices, bacon, fresh and cooked meat (on separate shelves), and salads and vegetables (except potatoes, which don't suit being stored in the cold). A refrigerator should be kept at an operating temperature of 4–5°C. It is worth investing in a refrigerator thermometer to ensure the correct temperature is maintained.

To ensure your refrigerator is functioning effectively for safe food storage, follow these guidelines:

To avoid bacterial cross-contamination, store cooked and raw foods on separate shelves, putting cooked foods on the top shelf. Ensure that all items are well wrapped.

Never put hot food into the refrigerator, as this will cause the internal temperature of the refrigerator to rise.

Avoid overfilling the refrigerator, as this restricts the circulation of air and can prevent the appliance from working properly.

It can take some time for the refrigerator to return to the correct operating temperature once the door has been opened, so don't leave it open any longer than is necessary.

Clean the refrigerator regularly, using a specially formulated germicidal refrigerator cleaner. Alternatively, use a weak solution of bicarbonate of soda: 1 tbsp to 1 litre (1¾ pints) water.

If your refrigerator doesn't have an automatic defrost facility, defrost regularly.

Maximum refrigerator storage times

For pre-packed foods, always adhere to the 'use by' date on the packet. For other foods, the following storage times should apply, providing the food is in prime condition when it goes into the refrigerator and that your refrigerator is in good working order:

Vegetables and fruit

Green vegetables	3–4 days
Salad leaves	2–3 days
Hard and stone fruit	3–7 days
Soft fruit	1–2 days

Dairy food

Cheese, hard	1 week
Cheese, soft	2–3 days
Eggs	1 week
Milk	4–5 days

Fish

Fish	1 day
Shellfish	1 day

Raw meat

Bacon	7 days
Game	2 days
Minced meat	1 day
Offal	1 day
Poultry	2 days
Raw sliced meat	2 days
Sausages	3 days

Cooked meat

Pies	2 days
Sliced meat	2 days
Ham	2 days
Ham, vacuum-packed (or according to the instructions on the packet)	1–2 weeks

1

Soups

Without a Slow Cooker

In step 2, bring to the boil, then reduce the heat and simmer for 20 minutes until the potatoes are tender. Complete the recipe as directed from step 3.

25g (1oz) butter

1 onion, finely chopped

1 garlic clove, crushed

550g (1¼lb) leeks, trimmed and chopped

200g (7oz) floury potatoes, peeled and sliced

1.2 litres (2 pints) hot vegetable stock (see page 10)

crème fraîche and chopped chives to garnish

Leek and Potato Soup

1 Melt the butter in a pan over a gentle heat, and cook the onion for 10–15 minutes until soft. Add the garlic and cook for a further 1 minute. Add the leeks and cook for 5–10 minutes until softened. Add the potatoes and toss together with the leeks.

2 Pour in the hot stock and bring to the boil. Transfer the soup to the slow cooker, cover and cook for 3-4 hours on Low until the potatoes are tender.

3 Leave to cool a little, then whiz in batches in a blender or food processor until smooth.

4 Reheat before serving, garnished with crème fraîche and chives.

Serves 4	EASY		NUTRITIONAL INFORMATION	
	Preparation Time 10 minutes	**Cooking Time** 30 minutes in pan then 3-4 hours on Low	**Per Serving** 117 calories, 6g fat (of which 4g saturates), 13g carbohydrate, 0.1g salt	Vegetarian Gluten Free

Without a Slow Cooker

In step 2, bring to the boil, then reduce the heat and simmer gently, uncovered, for 20–30 minutes. Complete the recipe as directed from step 3.

French Onion Soup

75g (3oz) butter
700g (11/2lb) onions, sliced
3 garlic cloves, crushed
1 tbsp plain flour
200ml (7fl oz) dry white wine
1 litre (1 3/4pints) hot vegetable stock (see page 10)
bouquet garni (see Cook's Tip)
salt and ground black pepper
1 small baguette, cut into slices 1cm (1/2in) thick
50g (2oz) Gruyère cheese or Cheddar, grated, to serve

1 Melt the butter in a large pan. Add the onions and cook slowly over a very low heat, stirring frequently, until very soft and golden brown; this should take at least 30 minutes. Add the garlic and flour and cook, stirring, for 1 minute.

2 Pour in the wine and let bubble until reduced by half. Add the stock, bouquet garni and seasoning. Bring to the boil, transfer to the slow cooker, cover and cook on low for 3-4 hours until the onions are meltingly tender.

3 Preheat the grill. Lightly toast the slices of baguette on both sides. Reheat the soup and adjust the seasoning. Discard the bouquet garni.

4 Divide the soup among four ovenproof soup bowls. Float two or three slices of toast on each portion and sprinkle thickly with the grated cheese. Stand the bowls under a hot grill until the cheese has melted and turned golden brown. Serve at once.

EASY		NUTRITIONAL INFORMATION		Serves
Preparation Time 30 minutes	**Cooking Time** 40 minutes in pan then 3–4 hours on low	**Per Serving** 438 calories, 21.2g fat (of which 13.2g saturates), 45.4g carbohydrate, 1.3g salt	Vegetarian	**4**

Cook's Tip

Lime Butter

Beat the grated zest and juice of ½ lime into 50g (2oz) softened butter and season to taste with salt and pepper. Shape into a log, wrap in clingfilm and chill until needed. To serve, unwrap and slice thinly.

Without a Slow Cooker

At the end of step 2, leave the mixture in the pan and bring to the boil. Reduce the heat, cover the pan and simmer gently for 20 minutes. Complete the recipe as directed from step 3.

Mexican Bean Soup

4 tbsp olive oil

1 onion, chopped

2 garlic cloves, chopped

pinch of crushed red chillies

1 tsp ground coriander

1 tsp ground cumin

½ tsp ground cinnamon

600ml (1 pint) hot vegetable stock (see page 10)

300ml (½ pint) tomato juice

1–2 tsp chilli sauce

2 x 400g cans red kidney beans, drained and rinsed

2 tbsp freshly chopped coriander

salt and ground black pepper

coriander leaves, roughly torn, to garnish

lime butter to serve (optional, see Cook's Tip)

1 Heat the oil in a large pan, add the onion, garlic, chillies and spices and fry gently for 5 minutes or until lightly golden.

2 Add the hot stock, the tomato juice, chilli sauce and beans and bring to the boil, then transfer to the slow cooker, cover and cook on High for 2–3 hours.

3 Leave the soup to cool a little, then whiz in batches in a blender or food processor until very smooth. Pour the soup into a pan, stir in the chopped coriander and heat through, then season to taste with salt and pepper.

4 Ladle the soup into warmed bowls. Top each portion with a few slices of lime butter, if you like, and scatter with torn coriander leaves.

Serves 6	EASY		NUTRITIONAL INFORMATION	
	Preparation Time 15 minutes	**Cooking Time** 10 minutes in pan then 2–3 hours on High	**Per Serving** (without lime butter) 184 calories, 8g fat (of which 1g saturates), 21g carbohydrate, 1.3g salt	Vegetarian Gluten Free

Lettuce Soup

50g (2oz) butter
350g (12oz) lettuce leaves, roughly chopped
125g (4oz) spring onions, trimmed and roughly chopped
1 tbsp plain wholemeal flour
600ml (1 pint) vegetable stock (see page 10)
150ml (¼ pint) milk
salt and ground black pepper
soured cream to serve (optional)

1 Melt the butter in a deep saucepan, add the lettuce and spring onions and cook gently for about 15 minutes until very soft.

2 Stir in the flour and cook, stirring, for 1 minute, then add the stock. Bring to the boil, then reduce the heat, cover the pan and simmer for 1 hour.

3 Leave the soup to cool a little, when whiz in batches in a blender or food processor until smooth. Return to the rinsed-out pan and add the milk with salt and pepper to taste. Reheat to serving temperature.

4 Ladle into warmed bowls and finish with a swirl of soured cream, if you like.

EASY		NUTRITIONAL INFORMATION	Serves
Preparation Time 5 minutes	**Cooking Time** 1 hour 20 minutes	**Per Serving** 139 calories, 11.5g fat (of which 7.5g saturates), 6.5g carbohydrate, 0.3g salt	**4**

Without a Slow Cooker

In step 3, bring to the boil and leave the soup in the pan. Season with salt and pepper, then reduce the heat, cover the pan and simmer for about 20 minutes, until the vegetables are tender. Complete the recipe as directed from step 4.

Carrot and Coriander Soup

40g (1½oz) butter
175g (6oz) leeks, trimmed and sliced
450g (1lb) carrots, sliced
2 tsp ground coriander
1 tsp plain flour
1 litre (1¾ pints) hot vegetable stock (see page 10)
150ml (¼ pint) single cream
salt and ground black pepper
coriander leaves, roughly torn, to serve

1 Melt the butter in a large pan. Add the leeks and carrots, stir, then cover the pan and cook gently for 7–10 minutes until the vegetables begin to soften but not colour.

2 Stir in the ground coriander and flour and cook, stirring, for 1 minute.

3 Add the stock and bring to the boil, stirring. Season with salt and pepper, then transfer to the slow cooker and cook for 3–4 hours on High until the vegetables are tender.

4 Leave the soup to cool a little, then whiz in batches in a blender or food processor until quite smooth. Pour into a clean pan and stir in the cream. Adjust the seasoning and reheat gently on the hob; do not boil. Ladle into warmed bowls, scatter with torn coriander leaves and serve.

Serves 6	EASY		NUTRITIONAL INFORMATION	
	Preparation Time 15 minutes	**Cooking Time** 15 minutes in pan then 3–4 hours on High	**Per Serving** 140 calories, 11g fat (of which 7g saturates), 10g carbohydrate, 0.2g salt	Vegetarian Gluten Free

Cook's Tip

This can be two meals in one: a starter and a main course. The beef flavours the stock and is removed before serving. You can then divide up the meat and serve it with mashed potatoes, swedes or turnips.

Without a Slow Cooker

Follow step 1, also adding the marrow bone to the pan along with the beef. At the end of the step, do not drain but instead add the broth mix and simmer, partially covered, for 1½ hours, skimming occasionally. Add the vegetables and 600ml (1 pint) cold water and bring to the boil, then reduce the heat and summer for 30 minutes. Complete the recipe as directed from step 3.

Scotch Broth

1.4kg (3lb) piece beef skirt (ask your butcher for this)

300g (11oz) broth mix (to include pearl barley, red lentils, split peas and green peas), soaked according to the pack instructions

2 carrots, finely chopped

1 parsnip, finely chopped

2 onions, finely chopped

¼ white cabbage, finely chopped

1 leek, trimmed and finely chopped

1 piece marrow bone, about 350g (12oz)

½ tbsp salt

ground black pepper

2 tbsp freshly chopped parsley to serve

1 Put the beef into a large pan and cover with water. Slowly bring to the boil, then reduce the heat and simmer for 10 minutes, using a slotted spoon to remove any scum that comes to the surface. Drain.

2 Put the broth mix and all the vegetables into the slow cooker, then place the beef and marrow bone on top. Add 1.5 litres (2½ pints) boiling water – there should be enough to just cover the meat. Cover and cook on Low for 8–10 hours until the meat is tender.

3 Remove the marrow bone and beef from the broth. Add a few shreds of beef to the broth, if you like. Season the broth well with the salt and some pepper, stir in the chopped parsley and serve hot.

EASY		NUTRITIONAL INFORMATION		Serves
Preparation Time 15 minutes	**Cooking Time** 15 minutes in pan then 8–10 hours on Low	**Per Serving** 173 calories, 2g fat (of which trace saturates), 35g carbohydrate, 2.3g salt	Dairy Free	**8**

Parsnip Soup with Chorizo

40g (1½oz) butter

1 onion, roughly chopped

225g (8oz) floury potatoes, such as King Edward, peeled and chopped

400g (14oz) parsnips, chopped

4 tsp paprika, plus extra to dust

1.1 litres (2 pints) vegetable stock (see page 10)

450ml (¾ pint) milk

4 tbsp double cream

75g (3oz) sliced chorizo sausage, cut into fine strips

salt and ground black pepper

parsnip crisps and freshly grated Parmesan to serve

1 Melt the butter in a large heavy-based pan over a gentle heat. Add the onion and cook for 15 minutes or until soft. Add the potatoes, parsnips and paprika. Mix well and cook gently, stirring occasionally, for 20 minutes or until the vegetables begin to soften.

2 Add the stock, milk and cream and season with salt and pepper. Bring to the boil, then reduce the heat and simmer for about 30 minutes or until the vegetables are very soft. Add 50g (2oz) of the chorizo. Allow the soup to cool a little, then whiz in a blender or food processor until smooth. The soup can be thinned with additional stock or milk, if you like. Check the seasoning and put back in the pan.

3 To serve, reheat the soup. Serve in warmed bowls and top each with parsnip crisps. Sprinkle with the remaining chorizo and a little Parmesan, and dust with paprika.

Freezing Tip

- -

To freeze Complete the recipe to the end of step 2, then cool, pack and freeze for up to one month.

To use Thaw the soup overnight at cool room temperature, then complete the recipe.

Serves 8	EASY		NUTRITIONAL INFORMATION	
	Preparation Time 20 minutes	**Cooking Time** 1 hour 15 minutes	**Per Serving** 278 calories, 20g fat (of which 9g saturates), 18g carbohydrate, 0.7g salt	Gluten Free

Cook's Tip

Dried peas form the base of this comforting soup. First, you need to soak them overnight in about 1 litre (1¾ pints) cold water. If you forget, put them straight into a pan with the water, bring to the boil and cook for 1–2 minutes, then leave to stand for 2 hours before using.

Without a Slow Cooker

At the end of step 2, leave the soup in the pan, reduce the heat and simmer, covered, for 45 minutes–1 hour or until the peas are very soft. Complete the recipe as directed from step 3.

Split Pea and Ham Soup

1 x 500g pack dried yellow split peas, soaked overnight (see Cook's Tip)

25g (1oz) butter

1 large onion, finely chopped

125g (4oz) rindless smoked streaky bacon rashers, roughly chopped

1 garlic clove, crushed

1.7 litres (3 pints) well-flavoured ham or vegetable stock

1 bouquet garni (see page 127)

1 tsp dried oregano

125g (4oz) cooked ham, chopped

salt and ground black pepper

cracked black pepper to serve

1 Drain the soaked split peas. Melt the butter in a large pan, add the onion, bacon and garlic and cook over a low heat for about 10 minutes or until the onion is soft.

2 Add the drained split peas to the pan with the stock. Bring to the boil and use a slotted spoon to remove any scum that comes to the surface. Add the bouquet garni and oregano, then season with salt and pepper. Transfer to the slow cooker, cover and cook on High for 3–4 hours until the peas are very soft.

3 Leave the soup to cool a little, then whiz half the soup in a blender or food processor until smooth. Pour the soup into a pan and reheat, then add the ham and check the seasoning. Ladle into warmed bowls and sprinkle with cracked black pepper to serve.

Serves 6	EASY		NUTRITIONAL INFORMATION	
	Preparation Time 15 minutes, plus overnight soaking	**Cooking Time** 15 minutes in pan then 3–4 hours on High	**Per Serving** 400 calories, 10g fat (of which 5g saturates), 53g carbohydrate, 1.5g salt	Gluten Free

Cock-a-Leekie Soup

1 oven-ready chicken, about 1.4kg (3lb),
ideally with giblets

2 onions, roughly chopped

2 carrots, roughly chopped

2 celery sticks, trimmed and roughly chopped

1 bay leaf

25g (1oz) butter

900g (2lb) leeks, trimmed and sliced

125g (4oz) ready-to-eat stoned prunes, sliced

salt and ground black pepper

freshly chopped parsley to serve

For the dumplings

125g (4oz) self-raising white flour

pinch of salt

50g (2oz) shredded suet

2 tbsp freshly chopped parsley

2 tbsp freshly chopped thyme

1 Put the chicken into a pan in which it fits quite snugly. Add the chopped vegetables, bay leaf and chicken giblets (if available). Add 1.7 litres (3 pints) water and bring to the boil, then reduce the heat, cover the pan and simmer gently for 1 hour.

2 Meanwhile, melt the butter in a large pan, add the leeks and fry gently for 10 minutes or until softened.

3 Remove the chicken from the pan. Strain the stock and set aside. Strip the chicken from the bones and shred roughly. Add to the broth with the prunes and softened leeks.

4 To make the dumplings, sift the flour and salt into a bowl. Stir in the suet, herbs and about 5 tbsp water to make a fairly firm dough. Lightly shape the dough into 2.5cm (1in) balls. Bring the soup just to the boil and season well. Reduce the heat, add the dumplings and cover the pan with a lid. Simmer for about 15–20 minutes until the dumplings are light and fluffy. Serve scattered with chopped parsley.

EASY		NUTRITIONAL INFORMATION	Serves
Preparation Time 30–40 minutes	**Cooking Time** 1 hour 20 minutes	**Per Serving** 280 calories, 4g fat (of which 1g saturates), 40g carbohydrate, 0.2g salt	**8**

Goulash Soup

700g (1½lb) silverside or lean chuck steak

25g (1oz) butter

225g (8oz) onions, chopped

1 small green pepper, seeded and chopped

4 tomatoes, skinned and quartered

150g (5oz) tomato purée

600ml (1 pint) rich beef stock (see page 10)

1 tbsp paprika

450g (1lb) potatoes, peeled

150ml (¼ pint) soured cream

salt and ground black pepper

freshly chopped parsley to garnish (optional)

1 Wipe the meat with a damp cloth. Remove any excess fat or gristle and cut the meat into small pieces. Season well with 2 tsp salt and pepper to taste.

2 Melt the butter in a large pan, add the onions and green pepper and sauté until tender.

3 Add the meat pieces, tomatoes, tomato purée, stock and paprika. Stir well and bring to the boil, then reduce the heat, cover the pan and simmer for 2½ hours, stirring occasionally.

4 Half an hour before the end of cooking, cut the potatoes into bite-sized pieces, bring to the boil in lightly salted water and simmer until cooked. Drain well and add to the soup.

5 Check the seasoning and stir in 2 tbsp soured cream. Ladle into warmed bowls, garnish with chopped parsley, if you like, and serve the remaining soured cream separately, for each person to spoon into their soup.

Serves	EASY		NUTRITIONAL INFORMATION	
6	**Preparation Time** 20 minutes	**Cooking Time** 2¾ hours	**Per Serving** 594 calories, 30g fat (of which 15g saturates), 35.5g carbohydrate, 1.9g salt	Gluten Free

125g (4oz) chana dal

1 tsp cumin seeds

2 tsp coriander seeds

1 tsp fenugreek seeds

3 dried red chillies

1 tbsp shredded coconut

2 tbsp ghee or polyunsaturated oil

225g (8oz) tomatoes, skinned and roughly chopped

½ tsp turmeric

1 tsp treacle

coriander sprigs to garnish

Spiced Dal Soup

1 Pick over the dal and remove any grit or discoloured pulses. Put into a sieve and wash in cold running water, then drain well and put into a pan. Cover with 600ml (1 pint) water and bring to the boil, then reduce the heat, cover the pan and simmer for 1 hour or until tender.

2 Put the cumin, coriander, fenugreek, chillies and coconut into a small electric mill or blender and grind finely. Heat the oil in a heavy-based frying pan, add the spice mixture and fry, stirring, for 30 seconds. Whiz the dal to a purée in a blender or food processor and put into a pan. Stir in the remaining ingredients and 300ml (½ pint) water.

3 Bring to the boil, then reduce the heat, cover the pan and simmer for about 20 minutes. Taste and adjust the seasoning. To serve, ladle into warmed bowls and garnish with coriander sprigs.

EASY		NUTRITIONAL INFORMATION		Serves
Preparation Time 5 minutes	**Cooking Time** 1½ hours	**Per Serving** 172 calories, 8.1g fat (of which 5g saturates), 19g carbohydrate, 0.2g salt	Vegetarian Gluten free	**4**

Beetroot Soup

750g (1lb 10oz) raw beetroot
1 tbsp olive oil
1 onion, finely chopped
275g (10oz) potatoes, peeled and roughly chopped
1.5 litres (2½ pints) hot vegetable stock (see page 10)
juice of 1 lemon
salt and ground black pepper

To serve
125ml (4fl oz) soured cream
25g (1oz) mixed root vegetable crisps (optional)
2 tbsp snipped chives

1 Peel the beetroot and cut into 1cm (½in) cubes. Heat the olive oil in a large pan. Add the onion and cook for 5 minutes to soften. Add the beetroot and potatoes and cook for a further 5 minutes.

2 Add the stock and lemon juice, and bring to the boil. Season with salt and pepper, transfer to the slow cooker and cook on high for 3-4 hours until the beetroot is tender. Cool slightly, then whiz in a blender or food processor until smooth.

3 Pour the soup into a clean pan and reheat gently on the hob. Divide the soup among warmed bowls. Swirl 1 tbsp soured cream on each portion, scatter with a few vegetable crisps if you like, and sprinkle with snipped chives to serve.

Without a Slow Cooker

In step 2, after bringing to the boil, leave the mixture in the pan, reduce the heat and simmer gently, half-covered, for 25 minutes. Leave to cool a little, then whiz in a blender or food processor until smooth. Complete the recipe as directed from step 3.

Freezing Tip

To freeze Complete the recipe to the end of step 2, then cool half or all the soup, pack and freeze for up to three months.
To use Thaw the soup overnight and simmer over a low heat for 5 minutes.

EASY		NUTRITIONAL INFORMATION		Serves
Preparation Time 15 minutes	**Cooking Time** 15 minutes in pan then 3-4 hours on High	**Per Serving** 290 calories, 25g fat (of which 4g saturates), 15g carbohydrate, 0.2g salt	Vegetarian Gluten free	**8**

2

Poultry

Chicken with Chorizo and Beans

1 tbsp olive oil

12 chicken pieces (6 drumsticks and 6 thighs)

175g (6oz) chorizo sausage, cubed

1 onion, finely chopped

2 large garlic cloves, crushed

1 tsp mild chilli powder

3 red peppers, seeded and roughly chopped

400g (14oz) passata (See Cook's Tip on page 41)

2 tbsp tomato purée

150ml (¼ pint) hot chicken stock (see page 11)

2 x 400g cans butter beans, drained and rinsed

200g (7oz) new potatoes, quartered

small bunch of thyme

1 bay leaf

200g (7oz) baby leaf spinach

1 Heat the oil in a large pan over a medium heat. Add the chicken and fry until browned all over, then transfer to the slow cooker.

2 Add the chorizo to the pan and fry for 2–3 minutes until its oil starts to run. Add the onion, garlic and chilli powder and fry over a low heat for 5 minutes or until the onion is soft.

3 Add the red peppers and cook for 2–3 minutes until soft. Stir in the passata, tomato purée, hot stock, butter beans, potatoes, thyme sprigs and bay leaf. Bring to the boil, then add to the chicken. Cover and cook on Low for 4–5 hours until the chicken is cooked through.

4 Remove the thyme and bay leaf, then stir in the spinach until it wilts. Serve immediately.

Without a Slow Cooker

Preheat the oven to 190°C (170°C fan oven) mark 5. At the end of step 1, transfer the chicken to a plate, then complete step 2. Add all the ingredients as described in step 3, cover and simmer for 10 minutes. Return the chicken to the pan, bring to a simmer, then pour everything into an ovenproof casserole with a lid and cook for 30–35 minutes in the oven. Complete step 4 to finish the recipe.

Serves 6	EASY		NUTRITIONAL INFORMATION	
	Preparation Time 10 minutes	**Cooking Time** 30 minutes in pan then 4–5 hours on Low	**Per Serving** 690 calories, 41g fat (of which 12g saturates), 33g carbohydrate, 2.6g salt	Gluten Free Dairy Free

Without a Slow Cooker

Complete step 1, setting the chicken aside on a plate. At the end of step 2, return the chicken to the pan, add the rice and one-third of the stock, then mix well and simmer until the liquid has been absorbed. Add the rest of the stock, along with the peas, bring to the boil, then reduce the heat to low and cook for 15–20 minutes until no liquid remains. Complete step 4 to finish the recipe.

1 tsp ground turmeric

1.1 litres (2 pints) hot chicken stock (see page 11)

2 tbsp vegetable oil

4 boneless, skinless chicken thighs, roughly diced

1 onion, chopped

1 red pepper, seeded and sliced

50g (2oz) chorizo sausage, diced

2 garlic cloves, crushed

300g (11oz) long-grain rice

125g (4oz) frozen peas

salt and ground black pepper

3 tbsp chopped flat-leafed parsley to garnish

crusty bread to serve

Spanish Chicken

1 Add the turmeric to the hot stock and leave to infuse for at least 5 minutes. Meanwhile, heat the oil in a large frying pan over a medium heat. Add the chicken and fry for 10 minutes or until golden, then transfer to the slow cooker.

2 Add the onion to the pan and cook over a medium heat for 5 minutes or until soft. Add the red pepper and chorizo and cook for a further 5 minutes, then add the garlic and cook for 1 minute.

3 Add the rice and mix well. Pour in the stock and peas and season, then transfer to the slow cooker and stir together. Cover and cook on Low for 1–2 hours until the rice is tender and the chicken is cooked through.

4 Check the seasoning and garnish with the parsley. Serve with some crusty bread.

Serves	EASY		NUTRITIONAL INFORMATION	
4	**Preparation Time** 25 minutes, plus infusing	**Cooking Time** 20 minutes in pan then 1–2 hours on Low	**Per Serving** 671 calories, 28g fat (of which 5g saturates), 70g carbohydrate, 0.8g salt	Gluten Free Dairy Free

Without a Slow Cooker

Preheat the oven to 180°C (160°C fan oven) mark 4. Put all the ingredients except the oil and the beans in a large, flameproof casserole, bring to the boil, then cook in the oven for 45 minutes. Test if the chicken is cooked as described in step 2. Add the beans and cook for 5 minutes, then complete step 3 to finish the recipe.

Try Something Different

Omit the baby new potatoes and serve with mashed potatoes.

Easy Chicken Casserole

1 tbsp sunflower oil
1 small chicken, about 1.4kg (3lb)
1 fresh rosemary sprig
2 bay leaves
1 red onion, cut into wedges
2 carrots, cut into chunks
2 leeks, trimmed and cut into chunks
2 celery sticks, trimmed and cut into chunks
12 baby new potatoes, halved if large
900ml (1½ pints) hot chicken stock (see page 11)
200g (7oz) green beans, trimmed
salt and ground black pepper

1 Heat the oil in a large pan over a medium heat. Add the chicken and fry until browned all over. Put the chicken into the slow cooker, along with the herbs and all the vegetables except the green beans. Season well.

2 Pour in the hot stock, cover and cook on Low for 5–6 hours until the chicken is cooked through. Add the beans for the last hour or cook separately in lightly salted boiling water and stir into the casserole once it's cooked. To test the chicken is cooked, pierce the thickest part of the leg with a knife: the juices should run clear.

3 Remove the chicken and spoon the vegetables into six bowls. Carve the chicken and divide among the bowls, then ladle the cooking liquid over.

EASY		NUTRITIONAL INFORMATION		Serves
Preparation Time 15 minutes	**Cooking Time** 10 minutes in pan then 5–6 hours on Low	**Per Serving** 323 calories, 18g fat (of which 5g saturates), 17g carbohydrate, 0.9g salt	Gluten Free Dairy Free	**6**

Garlic and Rosemary Roast Chicken

1.4kg (3lb) oven-ready chicken

4 tbsp freshly chopped rosemary or 1 tbsp dried rosemary

450g (1lb) each red and yellow peppers, quartered and seeded

450g (1lb) courgettes, cut into wedges or halved lengthways if small

125g (4oz) pitted black olives

2 tbsp capers

2 garlic cloves

50ml (2fl oz) olive oil

125g (4oz) streaky bacon or pancetta

2 tsp cornflour

300ml (½ pint) white wine

300ml (½ pint) chicken stock (see page 11)

salt and ground black pepper

fresh flat-leafed parsley to garnish

1 Preheat the oven to 200°C (180°C fan oven) mark 6. Fill the chicken cavity with half the rosemary.

2 Put the peppers, courgettes, black olives, capers, garlic, oil and seasoning into a roasting tin. Cover the chicken with the remaining rosemary and the streaky bacon or pancetta and sit it on the vegetables. Season and cover the chicken with foil.

3 Cook in the oven for 1(¼ hours, removing the foil halfway through the cooking time, until the chicken is cooked and the juices run clear when the thickest part of the thigh is pierced with a skewer.

4 Put the chicken and vegetables on a warmed serving plate and cover with foil to keep warm. Leave the garlic in the roasting tin with the cooking juices.

5 Mix the cornflour to a paste with 2 tbsp white wine. Add to the roasting tin with the remaining wine, the stock and seasoning, mashing the garlic into the liquid with a fork. Bring to the boil, stirring, then bubble for 5 minutes or until lightly thickened. Adjust the seasoning and serve with the chicken. Garnish with parsley.

Try Something Different

Make with chicken breasts: prepare peppers and courgettes as step 2; put with the olives, capers, garlic and oil into a roasting tin. Preheat the oven to 200°C (180°C fan oven) mark 6 and cook for 30–35 minutes. Add six chicken breasts. Snip the bacon and sprinkle it over the portions with the rosemary. Roast in the oven for 25–30 minutes. Remove the chicken and vegetables. Complete the gravy as steps 4 and 5.

EASY		NUTRITIONAL INFORMATION		Serves
Preparation Time 10 minutes	**Cooking Time** 1 hour 20 minutes, plus resting	**Per Serving** 700 calories, 47g fat (of which 13g saturates), 18g carbohydrate, 2.3g salt	Dairy Free	**4–6**

Alsace Chicken

2 tbsp vegetable oil

8 chicken pieces (such as breasts, thighs and drumsticks)

125g (4oz) rindless smoked streaky bacon rashers, cut into strips

12 shallots, peeled but left whole

3 fresh tarragon sprigs

1 tbsp plain flour

150ml (¼ pint) Alsace Riesling white wine

500ml (18fl oz) hot chicken stock (see page 11)

3 tbsp crème fraîche

salt and ground black pepper

new potatoes (optional) and green beans to serve

1 Heat half the oil in a frying pan over a medium heat. Fry the chicken, in batches, until golden, adding more oil to the pan as necessary. Set aside.

2 Put the bacon into the same pan and fry gently to release its fat. Add the shallots and cook for 5 minutes, stirring occasionally, or until both the shallots and bacon are lightly coloured.

3 Strip the leaves from the tarragon and put both the leaves and stalks to one side. Sprinkle the flour over the shallots and bacon and stir to absorb the juices. Cook for 1 minute, then gradually add the wine, hot stock and tarragon stalks. Put the chicken back into the pan, cover and simmer over a gentle heat for 45 minutes–1 hour until the chicken is cooked through.

4 Remove the chicken, bacon and shallots with a slotted spoon and keep warm. Discard the tarragon stalks. Bubble the sauce until reduced by half. Stir in the crème fraîche and tarragon leaves. Season with salt and pepper.

5 Turn off the heat, put the chicken, bacon and shallots back into the pan and stir to combine. Serve with new potatoes and green beans.

Serves 4	EASY		NUTRITIONAL INFORMATION
	Preparation Time 20 minutes	**Cooking Time** 1 hour 20 minutes	**Per Serving** 484 calories, 24g fat (of which 8g saturates), 11g carbohydrate, 1.4g salt

900g (2lb) floury potatoes, such as Maris Piper, peeled and cut into chunks

2 tbsp sweet paprika

1 tbsp ground coriander

large pinch of saffron threads, crushed

1 tsp each ground ginger and ground cinnamon

1 head of garlic, plus 2 crushed cloves

juice of ½ orange, plus 1 orange, cut into wedges

2 tbsp olive oil

1.4kg (3lb) oven-ready chicken

1 small onion, halved

2 red peppers, seeded and cut into eighths

75g (3oz) pinenuts

salt and ground black pepper

Spicy Roast Chicken with Red Peppers

1 Preheat the oven to 190°C (170°C fan oven) mark 5. Put the potatoes into a large pan of lightly salted cold water and bring to the boil. Cook for 5 minutes.

2 Meanwhile, put the paprika, coriander, saffron, ginger, cinnamon, two crushed garlic cloves, orange juice and oil into a bowl. Add ½ tsp each of salt and pepper and mix well. Put the chicken into a roasting tin and push the orange wedges and onion into the cavity. Season well, then rub the spice mix all over the chicken.

3 Drain the potatoes and shake in a colander to roughen their edges. Put around the chicken. Add the head of garlic and peppers and roast in the oven for 1 hour 20 minutes or until cooked.

4 About 10 minutes before the end of cooking, sprinkle the pinenuts over the chicken. Continue to cook until the juices run clear when the thickest part of the thigh is pierced with a skewer. Carve and serve with the vegetables.

EASY		NUTRITIONAL INFORMATION		Serves
Preparation Time 30 minutes	**Cooking Time** about 1½ hours	**Per Serving** 787 calories, 49g fat (of which 11g saturates), 45g carbohydrate, 0.5g salt	Gluten Free Dairy Free	**4**

Classic Coq au Vin

1 large chicken, jointed, (see page 14)
or 6–8 chicken joints

2 tbsp well-seasoned flour

100g (3½oz) butter

125g (4oz) lean bacon, diced

1 medium onion, quartered

1 medium carrot, quartered

4 tbsp brandy

600ml (1 pint) red wine

1 garlic clove, crushed

1 bouquet garni (see page 10)

1 sugar cube

2 tbsp vegetable oil

450g (1lb) button onions

pinch of sugar

1 tsp wine vinegar

225g (8oz) button mushrooms

6 slices white bread, crusts removed

salt and ground black pepper

1 Coat the chicken pieces with 1 tbsp seasoned flour. Melt 25g (1oz) butter in a flameproof casserole. Add the chicken and fry gently until golden brown on all sides. Add the bacon, onion and carrot and fry until softened.

2 Heat the brandy in a small pan, pour over the chicken and ignite, shaking the pan so that all the chicken pieces are covered in flames. Pour in the wine and stir to dislodge any sediment from the base of the casserole. Add the garlic, bouquet garni and sugar cube and bring to the boil. Reduce the heat, cover and simmer for 1–1½ hours or until the chicken is cooked through.

3 Meanwhile, melt 25g (1oz) butter with 1 tsp oil in a frying pan. Add the button onions and fry until they begin to brown. Add the pinch of sugar and vinegar together with 1 tbsp water. Cover and simmer for 10–15 minutes until just tender. Keep warm.

4 Melt 25g (1oz) butter with 2 tsp oil in a pan. Add the mushrooms and cook for a few minutes, then turn off the heat and keep warm.

5 Remove the chicken from the casserole and place in a dish. Surround with the onions and mushrooms and keep hot.

6 Discard the bouquet garni. Skim the excess fat from the cooking liquid, then boil the liquid in the casserole briskly for 3–5 minutes to reduce it.

7 Add the remaining oil to the fat in the frying pan and fry the pieces of bread until golden brown on both sides. Cut each slice into triangles.

8 Work the remaining butter and flour to make a beurre manié. Remove the casserole from the heat and add small pieces of the beurre manié to the liquid. Stir until smooth, then put back on to the heat and bring just to the boil. The sauce should be thick and shiny. Take off the heat and adjust the seasoning. Return the chicken, onions and mushrooms to the casserole and stir to combine. Serve with the fried bread.

Serves 6	A LITTLE EFFORT		NUTRITIONAL INFORMATION
	Preparation Time 15 minutes	**Cooking Time** 2 hours 10 minutes	**Per Serving** 740 calories, 44g fat (of which 17g saturates), 26g carbohydrate, 1.8g salt

Exotic Chicken

1 large red chilli, seeded and finely chopped (see page 9)

2.5cm (1in) piece fresh root ginger, peeled and thinly sliced

10cm (4in) piece lemongrass, cut into thin matchsticks

2 kaffir lime leaves, cut into thin matchsticks (or a little extra grated lime zest)

grated zest of 1 lime and juice of 2

2 garlic bulbs, halved

2 tbsp freshly chopped coriander

1.8kg (4lb) oven-ready chicken

1 tbsp chilli sauce

3 tbsp rapeseed oil

1 tsp ground turmeric

800g (1¾lb) baby new potatoes

3 tbsp desiccated coconut

salt and ground black pepper

fresh coriander to garnish

1 Preheat the oven to 200°C (180°C fan oven) mark 6. Cut two pieces of non-stick baking parchment, each measuring about 75 x 40cm (30 x 16in). Sprinkle each with water to dampen slightly, then put one on top of the other.

2 Combine the chilli, ginger, lemongrass, kaffir lime leaves, some of the grated lime zest and the garlic with the coriander. Pile in the centre of the baking parchment. Season inside the chicken generously with salt and pepper, then scatter the rest of the grated lime zest over and put the chicken on top of the spices.

3 Mix the chilli sauce with 1 tbsp oil and brush all over the chicken. Bring the edges of the baking parchment together and tie at the top with kitchen string to encase the chicken completely. Put into a large roasting tin just big enough to hold the parcel and cook in the oven for 1 hour 40 minutes.

4 Mix the remaining oil with the turmeric and potatoes in a roasting tin and toss well to coat evenly. Put on a tray above the chicken for the last 40 minutes of the cooking time. Roast until golden and tender. Remove the potatoes from the oven, add the desiccated coconut and stir to coat evenly. Put back in the oven and cook for a further 5 minutes or until the coconut has turned golden. Keep warm.

5 Untie the parcel and allow any juices inside the chicken to run into a pan. Lift the chicken out and add as much of the flavouring ingredients as possible to the pan. Cover the chicken with foil and keep warm in a low oven. Add the lime juice to the pan and bring to the boil. Bubble furiously for 1 minute. Keep hot.

6 Carve the chicken and serve with the roast potatoes and cooking juices. Garnish with fresh coriander.

EASY		NUTRITIONAL INFORMATION		Serves
Preparation Time 20 minutes	**Cooking Time** 1¾ hours	**Per Serving** 370 calories, 17g fat (of which 6g saturates), 22g carbohydrate, 0.5g salt	Gluten Free Dairy Free	**6**

Without a Slow Cooker

Cook the tagine in a large, flameproof casserole. After step 1, transfer the chicken to a plate, complete step 2, then return the chicken to the casserole and add the ingredients as described at the start of step 3. Cover and bring to the boil, then simmer for 45 minutes until the chicken is falling off the bone. Garnish and serve as described.

Chicken Tagine

2 tbsp olive oil

4 chicken thighs

1 onion, chopped

2 tsp ground cinnamon

2 tbsp runny honey

150g (5oz) dried apricots

75g (3oz) blanched almonds

125ml (4fl oz) hot chicken stock (see page 11)

salt and ground black pepper

flaked almonds to garnish

couscous to serve

1 Heat 1 tbsp oil in a large pan over a medium heat. Add the chicken and fry for 5 minutes or until brown, then transfer to the slow cooker.

2 Add the onion to the pan with the remaining oil and fry for 10 minutes or until softened.

3 Add the cinnamon, honey, apricots, almonds and hot stock to the onion and season well. Bring to the boil, then transfer to the slow cooker, cover and cook on Low for 4–5 hours until the chicken is tender and cooked through. Garnish with the flaked almonds and serve hot with couscous.

Serves 4	EASY		NUTRITIONAL INFORMATION	
	Preparation Time 10 minutes	**Cooking Time** 20 minutes in the pan then 4–5 hours on Low	**Per Serving** 376 calories, 22g fat (of which 4g saturates), 19g carbohydrate, 0.5g salt	Gluten Free Dairy Free

2 limes, halved

1.4kg (3lb) oven-ready chicken

knob of butter

2 lemongrass stalks, crushed

450ml (¾ pint) dry white wine

450ml (¾ pint) chicken stock (see page 11)

small bunch of coriander, chopped

salt and ground black pepper

rice and vegetables to serve

Thai Poached Chicken

1 Preheat the oven to 200°C (180°C fan oven) mark 6. Put two lime halves into the cavity of the chicken. Rub the chicken with the butter and season with salt and pepper. Put the chicken into a flameproof casserole.

2 Add the lemongrass and remaining lime to the casserole, then pour in the wine and stock. Cover with a tight-fitting lid and cook in the oven for 1 hour.

3 Uncover and cook for a further 30 minutes or until the chicken is cooked and the juices run clear when the thickest part of the thigh is pierced with a skewer. Sprinkle the coriander over the chicken and serve with rice and vegetables.

EASY		NUTRITIONAL INFORMATION		Serves
Preparation Time 10 minutes	**Cooking Time** 1½ hours	**Per Serving** 579 calories, 36g fat (of which 10g saturates), 1g carbohydrate, 1g salt	Gluten Free Dairy Free	**4**

Turkey Crown with Orange

2 onions, sliced

2 bay leaves

2.7kg (6lb) oven-ready turkey crown

40g (1½oz) butter, softened

1 lemon, halved

2 tbsp chicken seasoning

2 oranges, halved

150ml (¼ pint) dry white wine or chicken stock (see page 11)

1 Preheat the oven to 190°C (170°C fan oven) mark 5. Spread the onions in a large roasting tin, add the bay leaves and sit the turkey on top. Spread the butter over the turkey breast, then squeeze the lemon over it. Put the lemon halves in the tin. Sprinkle the chicken seasoning over the turkey and then put the orange halves in the tin, around the turkey.

2 Pour the wine or stock into the roasting tin, with 250ml (9fl oz) hot water. Cover the turkey loosely with a large sheet of foil. Make sure it's completely covered, but with enough space between the foil and the turkey for air to circulate.

3 Roast in the oven for 2 hours or until the turkey is cooked through and the juices run clear when the thickest part of the thigh is pierced with a skewer. Remove the foil and put back in the oven for 30 minutes or until golden.

4 Lift the turkey on to a warmed carving dish, cover loosely with foil and leave to rest for 15 minutes before carving.

Serves 8	EASY		NUTRITIONAL INFORMATION	
	Preparation Time 20 minutes	**Cooking Time** 2½ hours, plus resting	**Per Serving** 181 calories, 6g fat (of which 3g saturates), 3g carbohydrate, 0.2g salt	Gluten Free

Goose with Roasted Apples

6 small red onions, halved

7 small red eating apples, unpeeled, halved

5kg (11lb) oven-ready goose, washed, dried and seasoned inside and out

small bunch of sage

small bunch of rosemary

1 bay leaf

salt and ground black pepper

For the gravy

1 tbsp plain flour

300ml (½ pint) red wine

200ml (7fl oz) giblet stock (see page 10)

1 Preheat the oven to 230°C (210°C fan oven) mark 8. Put half an onion and half an apple inside the goose with half the sage and rosemary and the bay leaf. Tie the legs together with string. Push a long skewer through the wings to tuck them in. Put the goose, breast side up, on a rack in a roasting tin. Prick the breast all over and season with salt and pepper. Put the remaining onions around the bird, then cover with foil.

2 Roast in the oven for 30 minutes, then remove the tin from the oven and baste the goose with the fat that has run off. Remove and set aside any excess fat. Reduce the oven temperature to 190°C (170°C fan oven) mark 5 and roast for a further 1½ hours, removing any excess fat every 20–30 minutes.

3 Remove the foil from the goose. Remove excess fat, then add the remaining apples. Sprinkle the goose with the remaining herbs and roast for a further 1 hour or until cooked. Test by piercing the thigh with a skewer – the juices should run clear. Remove the goose from the oven and put it on a warmed serving plate. Cover with foil and leave to rest for 30 minutes. Remove the apples and onions and keep warm.

4 To make the gravy, pour out all but 1 tbsp of the fat from the tin, stir in the flour, then add the wine and stock. Bring to the boil and cook, stirring, for 5 minutes. Carve the goose, cut the roast apples into wedges and serve with the goose, onions and gravy.

EASY		NUTRITIONAL INFORMATION		Serves
Preparation Time 30 minutes	**Cooking Time** 3 hours, plus resting	**Per Serving** 646 calories, 41g fat (of which 12g saturates), 11g carbohydrate, 1g salt	Dairy Free	**8**

3

Meat and Game

Mexican Chilli con Carne

Beef Goulash

Beef and Guinness Stew

Peppered Winter Stew

Beef with Beer and Mushrooms

Beef Casserole with Black Olives

Braised Beef with Pancetta and Mushrooms

Steak and Onion Puff Pie

Steak and Kidney Pie

Lamb, Prune and Almond Tagine

Stuffed Leg of Lamb

Curried Lamb with Lentils

Braised Lamb Shanks with Cannellini Beans

Lamb, Potato and Peanut Curry

Luxury Lamb and Leek Hotpot

Turkish Lamb Stew

Italian Braised Leg of Lamb

Pork and Apple Hotpot

One-pot Gammon Stew

Roast Pork Loin with Rosemary and Mustard

Spicy Pork and Bean Stew

Pheasant Casserole with Cider and Apples

Rabbit Casserole with Prunes

Mexican Chilli con Carne

2 tbsp olive oil

450g (1lb) minced beef

1 large onion, finely chopped

½–1 tsp each hot chilli powder and ground cumin

3 tbsp tomato purée

150ml (¼ pint) hot beef stock

1 x 400g can chopped tomatoes with garlic (see Cook's Tips)

25g (1oz) plain chocolate

1 x 400g can red kidney beans, drained and rinsed

2 x 20g packs coriander, chopped

salt and ground black pepper

guacamole, salsa, soured cream, grated cheese, tortilla chips and pickled chillies to serve

1 Heat 1 tbsp oil in a large pan and fry the beef for 10 minutes or until well browned, stirring to break up any lumps. Remove from the pan with a slotted spoon and transfer to the slow cooker.

2 Add the remaining oil to the pan, then fry the onion, stirring, for 10 minutes or until soft and golden.

3 Add the spices and fry for 1 minute, then add the tomato purée, hot stock and the tomatoes. Bring to the boil, then stir into the mince in the slow cooker. Cover and cook on Low for 4–5 hours.

4 Stir in the chocolate, kidney beans and coriander and season with salt and pepper, then leave to stand for 10 minutes.

5 Serve with guacamole, salsa, soured cream, grated cheese, tortilla chips and pickled chillies.

Without a Slow Cooker

Follow step 1, then transfer the beef to a plate and complete step 2. At the end of step 3, leave the mixture in the pan, return the beef to the pan and simmer, uncovered, for 35–40 minutes until thickened. Stir in the ingredients as described in step 4 and simmer for 5 minutes. Serve as described.

Serves	EASY		NUTRITIONAL INFORMATION	
4	**Preparation Time** 5 minutes	**Cooking Time** 25 minutes in pan then 4–5 hours on Low	**Per Serving** 408 calories, 19g fat (of which 7g saturates), 28g carbohydrate, 1.1g salt	Gluten Free Dairy Free

Without a Slow Cooker

Cook the recipe in a deep, flameproof casserole. Preheat the oven to 170°C (fan oven 150°C) mark 3. At the end of step 2, transfer the meat to a plate, then return it to the casserole at the end of step 3. Add the ingredients described in step 4, then bring to a simmer, cover tightly and cook in the oven for 1½ hours, topping up the liquid after 1 hour if necessary. Complete step 5 to finish the recipe.

1kg (2¼lb) stewing steak

2 tbsp seasoned plain flour

3 tbsp vegetable oil

700g (1½lb) onions, chopped

225g (8oz) pancetta cubes or bacon lardons

2 garlic cloves, crushed

4 tbsp paprika

2 tsp dried mixed herbs

1 x 400g can peeled plum tomatoes

150ml (¼ pint) hot beef stock (see page 10)

150ml (¼ pint) soured cream

salt and ground black pepper

chopped parsley, to garnish

noodles to serve

Beef Goulash

1 Cut the beef into 3cm (1¼in) cubes, then toss the cubes in the flour to coat and shake off any excess.

2 Heat 2 tbsp oil in a large pan and quickly fry the meat in small batches until browned on all sides. Transfer to the slow cooker.

3 Heat the remaining oil in the pan, add the onions and fry gently for 5–7 minutes until starting to soften and turn golden. Add the pancetta or lardons and fry over a high heat until crispy. Stir in the garlic and paprika and cook, stirring, for 1 minute.

4 Add the herbs, tomatoes and hot stock and bring to the boil. Stir into the beef in the slow cooker, cover and cook on Low for 8–10 hours until tender.

5 Check the seasoning, then stir in the soured cream. Garnish with parsley and serve with noodles.

Serves 6	EASY		NUTRITIONAL INFORMATION
	Preparation Time 30 minutes	**Cooking Time** 20 minutes in pan then 8–10 hours on Low	**Per Serving** 726 calories, 44g fat (of which 16g saturates), 21g carbohydrate, 1.6g salt

Beef and Guinness Stew

1.4kg (3lb) shin of beef or braising steak, cut into 3cm (1¼in) cubes

2 tbsp seasoned plain flour

4 tbsp vegetable oil

2 medium onions, sliced

4 medium carrots, cut into chunks

225ml (8fl oz) Guinness

300ml (½ pint) hot beef stock (see page 10)

2 bay leaves

700g (1½lb) baby potatoes, halved if large

2 tbsp freshly chopped flat-leafed parsley

salt and ground black pepper

1 Toss the beef in the flour to coat and shake off any excess. Heat the oil in a large pan until hot. Add a handful of beef and cook until well browned. Remove with a slotted spoon, transfer to the slow cooker and repeat until all the meat is browned.

2 Add the onions and carrots to the pan and cook for 10 minutes or until browned. Add the Guinness, scraping the base to loosen the goodness, then stir in the hot stock. Add the bay leaves and potatoes and bring to the boil. Pour over the beef in the slow cooker, cover and cook on Low for 8–10 hours until the meat is tender.

3 Stir in the parsley, season to taste and serve.

EASY		NUTRITIONAL INFORMATION		Serves
Preparation Time 15 minutes	**Cooking Time** 20 minutes in pan then 8–10 hours on Low	**Per Serving** 526 calories, 29g fat (of which 10g saturates), 10g carbohydrate, 0.4g salt	Dairy Free	**6**

Beef Casserole with Black Olives

6 tbsp oil

1.1kg (2½lb) stewing steak, cut into 4cm (1½in) cubes

350g (12oz) unsmoked streaky bacon rashers, rind removed and sliced into thin strips

450g (1lb) onions, roughly chopped

3 large garlic cloves

2 tbsp tomato purée

125ml (4fl oz) brandy

1 tbsp plain flour

150ml (¼ pint) red wine

300ml (½ pint) beef stock (see page 10)

1 bouquet garni (see page 10)

225g (8oz) flat mushrooms, quartered if large

125g (4oz) black olives

fresh flat-leafed parsley sprigs to garnish (optional)

1 Heat 3 tbsp oil in a large flameproof casserole over a high heat. Brown the steak in batches until dark chestnut brown, then remove from the pan and keep warm. Add the bacon and fry until golden brown, then put to one side with the beef.

2 Add the remaining oil and cook the onions over a medium heat for 10–15 minutes until golden. Add the garlic, fry for 30 seconds, then add the tomato purée and cook, stirring, for 1–2 minutes. Add the brandy.

3 Preheat the oven to 170°C (150°C fan oven) mark 3. Bring the casserole to the boil and bubble to reduce by half, then add the flour and mix until smooth. Pour in the wine, bring back to the boil and bubble for 1 minute. Put the steak and bacon back into the casserole, then add enough stock to barely cover the meat. Add the bouquet garni. Bring to the boil, then cover, put into the oven and cook for 1¼–1½ hours until the steak is tender. Add the mushrooms and cook for a further 4–5 minutes.

4 Just before serving, remove the bouquet garni and stir in the black olives. Serve hot, garnished with parsley, if you like.

Freezing Tip

To freeze Complete the recipe to the end of step 3. Cool quickly and put into a freezerproof container. Seal and freeze for up to one month.

To use Thaw overnight at cool room temperature. Preheat the oven to 180°C (160°C fan oven) mark 4. Bring slowly to the boil on the hob, then cover and reheat in the oven for 20–25 minutes. Complete the recipe.

EASY		NUTRITIONAL INFORMATION		Serves
Preparation Time 20 minutes	**Cooking Time** 2 hours 10 minutes	**Per Serving** 704 calories, 45g fat (of which 13g saturates), 9g carbohydrate, 3.3g salt	Dairy Free	**6**

Freezing Tip

To freeze Complete the recipe to the end of step 4, without the garnish. Put into a freezerproof container, cool and freeze for up to three months.
To use Thaw overnight at cool room temperature. Preheat the oven to 180°C (160°C fan oven) mark 4. Bring to the boil on the hob, cover tightly and reheat in the oven for about 30 minutes or until piping hot.

175g (6oz) smoked pancetta or smoked streaky bacon, cubed

2 leeks, trimmed and thickly sliced

1 tbsp olive oil

450g (1lb) braising steak, cut into 5cm (2in) pieces

1 large onion, finely chopped

2 carrots, thickly sliced

2 parsnips, thickly sliced

1 tbsp plain flour

300ml (½ pint) red wine

1–2 tbsp redcurrant jelly

125g (4oz) chestnut mushrooms, halved

ground black pepper

freshly chopped flat-leafed parsley to garnish

Braised Beef with Pancetta and Mushrooms

1 Preheat the oven to 170°C (150°C fan oven) mark 3. Fry the pancetta or bacon in a shallow flameproof casserole for 2–3 minutes until golden. Add the leeks and cook for a further 2 minutes or until they are just beginning to colour. Remove with a slotted spoon and set aside.

2 Heat the oil in the casserole. Fry the beef in batches for 2–3 minutes until golden brown on all sides. Remove and set aside. Add the onion and fry over a gentle heat for 5 minutes or until golden. Stir in the carrots and parsnips and fry for 1–2 minutes.

3 Put the beef back into the casserole and stir in the flour to soak up the juices. Gradually add the wine and 300ml (½ pint) water, then stir in the redcurrant jelly. Season with pepper and bring to the boil. Cover with a tight-fitting lid and cook in the oven for 2 hours.

4 Stir in the leeks, pancetta and mushrooms, cover and cook for a further 1 hour or until everything is tender. Serve hot, sprinkled with chopped parsley.

Serves 4	EASY		NUTRITIONAL INFORMATION	
	Preparation Time 20 minutes	**Cooking Time** about 3½ hours	**Per Serving** 541 calories, 25g fat (of which 9g saturates), 30g carbohydrate, 1.6g salt	Dairy Free

Freezing Tip

To freeze Complete the recipe to the end of step 3. Cool the casserole quickly. Put the beef mixture into a pie dish. Brush the dish edge with water, put on the pastry and press down lightly to seal. Score the pastry. Cover with clingfilm and freeze for up to three months.
To use Thaw overnight at cool room temperature or in the fridge. Lightly score the pastry, brush with beaten egg and cook at 220°C (200°C fan oven) mark 7 for 35 minutes or until the pastry is brown and the filling piping hot.

Steak and Onion Puff Pie

3 tbsp vegetable oil
2 onions, sliced
900g (2lb) casserole beef, cut into chunks
3 tbsp plain flour
500ml (18fl oz) hot beef stock (see page 10)
2 fresh rosemary sprigs, bruised
flour to dust
1 x 500g pack puff pastry
1 medium egg, beaten, to glaze
salt and ground black pepper

1 Preheat the oven to 170°C (150°C fan oven) mark 3.

2 Heat 1 tbsp oil in a large flameproof casserole and sauté the onions for 10 minutes or until golden. Lift out and put to one side. Sear the meat in the same casserole, in batches, using more oil as necessary, until brown all over. Lift out each batch as soon as it is browned and put to one side. Add the flour to the casserole and cook for 1–2 minutes to brown. Return the onions and beef to the casserole and add the hot stock and the rosemary. Season well with salt and pepper. Cover and bring to the boil, then cook in the oven for 1½ hours or until the meat is tender.

3 About 30 minutes before the end of the cooking time, lightly dust a worksurface with flour and roll out the pastry. Cut out a lid using a 1.1 litre (2 pint) pie dish as a template, or use four 300ml (½ pint) dishes and cut out four lids. Put on a baking sheet and chill.

4 Remove the casserole from the oven. Increase the heat to 220°C (200°C fan oven) mark 7. Pour the casserole into the pie dish (or dishes), brush the edge with water and put on the pastry lid. Press lightly to seal. Lightly score the top and brush with the egg. Put the dish back on the baking sheet. Bake for 30 minutes or until the pastry is risen and golden. Serve immediately.

EASY		NUTRITIONAL INFORMATION	Serves
Preparation Time 30 minutes	**Cooking Time** about 2½ hours	**Per Serving** 1036 calories, 67g fat (of which 10g saturates), 65g carbohydrate, 1.4g salt	**4**

Steak and Kidney Pie

700g (1½lb) stewing steak, cut into cubes and seasoned

2 tbsp plain flour, plus extra to dust

3 tbsp vegetable oil

25g (1oz) butter

1 small onion, finely chopped

175g (6oz) ox kidney, cut into small pieces

150g (5oz) flat mushrooms, cut into large chunks

small pinch of cayenne pepper

1 tsp anchovy essence

350g (12oz) puff pastry, thawed if frozen

1 large egg, beaten with a pinch of salt, to glaze

salt and ground black pepper

1 Preheat the oven to 170°C (150°C fan oven) mark 3. Toss half the steak with half the flour. Heat the oil in a flameproof non-stick casserole and add the butter. Fry the steak in batches until brown. Lift out each batch as soon as it is browned and put to one side.

2 Add the onion and cook gently until soft. Return the steak to the casserole with 200ml (7fl oz) water, the kidney, mushrooms, cayenne and anchovy essence. Bring to the boil, then cover the pan, reduce the heat and simmer for 5 minutes.

3 Transfer to the oven and cook for 1 hour or until tender. The sauce should be syrupy. If not, transfer the casserole to the hob, remove the lid, bring to the boil and bubble for 5 minutes to reduce the liquid. Leave the steak mixture to cool.

4 Turn up the oven to 200°C (180°C fan oven) mark 6. Put the steak and kidney mixture into a 900ml (1½ pint) pie dish. Pile it high to support the pastry lid.

5 Roll out the pastry on a lightly floured surface to 5mm (¼in) thick. Cut off four to six strips, 1cm (½in) wide. Dampen the edge of the dish with cold water, then press the pastry strips on to the edge. Dampen the pastry rim and lay the sheet of pastry on top. Press the surfaces together, trim the edge and press down with the back of a knife to seal. Brush the pastry with the egg glaze and score with the back of a knife. Put the pie dish on a baking sheet and cook for 30 minutes or until the pastry is golden brown and the filling is hot to the centre.

Serves 6	EASY		NUTRITIONAL INFORMATION
	Preparation Time 40 minutes, plus cooling	**Cooking Time** about 2 hours	**Per Serving** 565 calories, 36g fat (of which 8g saturates), 26g carbohydrate, 0.9g salt

Without a Slow Cooker

At the end of step 3, leave the mixture in the pan, bring to the boil, then reduce the heat, cover the pan and simmer for 1 hour. remove the lid and cook for 30 minutes, stirring occasionally, or until the sauce is thick and the lamb is tender. Complete step 4 to serve.

Curried Lamb with Lentils

500g (1lb 2oz) lean stewing lamb on the bone, cut into 8 pieces (ask your butcher to do this), trimmed of fat

1 tsp ground cumin

1 tsp ground turmeric

2 garlic cloves, crushed

1 medium red chilli, seeded and chopped (see page 19)

2.5cm (1in) piece fresh root ginger, peeled and grated

2 tbsp vegetable oil

1 onion, chopped

1 x 400g can chopped tomatoes

2 tbsp vinegar

175g (6oz) red lentils, rinsed

salt and ground black pepper

coriander sprigs to garnish

rocket salad to serve

1 Put the lamb into a shallow sealable container and add the spices, garlic, chilli, ginger, salt and pepper. Stir well to mix, then cover and chill for at least 30 minutes.

2 Heat the oil in a large pan, add the onion and cook over a low heat for 5 minutes. Add the lamb and cook for 10 minutes, turning regularly, or until the meat is evenly browned.

3 Add the tomatoes, vinegar, lentils and 225ml (8fl oz) boiling water and bring to the boil. Season well. Transfer to the slow cooker, cover and cook on Low for 5–6 hours until the lamb is tender.

4 Serve hot, garnished with coriander, with a rocket salad.

Serves	EASY		NUTRITIONAL INFORMATION	
4	**Preparation Time** 15 minutes, plus marinating	**Cooking Time** 20 minutes in pan then 5–6 hours on Low	**Per Serving** 478 calories, 22g fat (of which 7g saturates), 36g carbohydrate, 0.3g salt	Gluten Free Dairy Free

Braised Lamb Shanks with Cannellini Beans

3 tbsp olive oil
6 lamb shanks
1 large onion, chopped
3 carrots, sliced
3 celery sticks, trimmed and sliced
2 garlic cloves, crushed
2 x 400g cans chopped tomatoes
125ml (4fl oz) balsamic vinegar
2 bay leaves
2 x 400g cans cannellini beans, drained and rinsed
salt and ground black pepper

1 Preheat the oven to 170°C (150°C fan oven) mark 3. Heat the oil in a large flameproof casserole and brown the lamb shanks, in two batches, all over. Remove and set aside.

2 Add the onion, carrots, celery and garlic to the casserole and cook gently until softened and just beginning to colour.

3 Return the lamb to the casserole and add the chopped tomatoes and balsamic vinegar, giving the mixture a good stir. Season with salt and pepper and add the bay leaves. Bring to a simmer, cover and cook on the hob for 5 minutes.

4 Transfer to the oven and cook for 1½–2 hours or until the lamb shanks are nearly tender.

5 Remove the casserole from the oven and add the cannellini beans. Cover and return to the oven for a further 30 minutes, then serve.

EASY		NUTRITIONAL INFORMATION		Serves
Preparation Time 15 minutes	**Cooking Time** 3 hours	**Per Serving** 382 calories, 18g fat (of which 6g saturates), 29g carbohydrate, 1.2g salt	Gluten Free Dairy free	**6**

Cook's Tip

Massaman paste is a Thai curry paste. The ingredients include red chillies, roasted shallots, roasted garlic, galangal, lemongrass, roasted coriander seeds, roasted cumin, roasted cloves, white pepper, salt and shrimp paste. It's available in supermarkets or Asian food stores.

Lamb, Potato and Peanut Curry

2 tbsp olive oil

1 medium onion, chopped

1 tbsp peeled and grated fresh root ginger

1.6kg (3¹/₂lb) leg of lamb, diced

3–4 tbsp Massaman paste (see Cook's Tip)

1 tbsp fish sauce

2 tbsp peanut butter

100g (3¹/₂oz) ground almonds

1 x 400ml can coconut milk

600ml (1 pint) hot chicken stock (see page 11)

1–2 tbsp dry sherry

500g (1lb 2oz) small potatoes, peeled and quartered

200g (7oz) green beans, trimmed

75g (3oz) toasted peanuts, roughly chopped

1 x 20g pack coriander, finely chopped

2 limes, quartered

rice to serve

1 Preheat the oven to 170°C (150°C fan oven) mark 3. Heat the oil in a large flameproof casserole. Add the onion and cook over a medium heat for 7–8 minutes until golden. Add the ginger and cook for 1 minute. Spoon the onion mixture out of the pan and set aside. Add the lamb and fry in batches until browned. Put to one side.

2 Add the Massaman paste, fish sauce and peanut butter to the casserole and fry for 2–3 minutes, then add the reserved onion and ginger mixture, lamb pieces, the ground almonds, coconut milk, hot stock and sherry.

3 Bring to the boil, then cover with a lid and cook in the oven for 1 hour. Add the potatoes and cook for a further 40 minutes, uncovered, adding the green beans for the last 20 minutes. Garnish with toasted peanuts and coriander. Serve with freshly cooked rice and lime wedges to squeeze over the curry.

Serves 8	EASY		NUTRITIONAL INFORMATION	
	Preparation Time 20 minutes	**Cooking Time** about 2 hours	**Per Serving** 664 calories, 47g fat (of which 20g saturates), 19g carbohydrate, 0.5g salt	Gluten Free Dairy Free

Luxury Lamb and Leek Hotpot

50g (2oz) butter
400g (14oz) leeks, sliced
1 medium onion, chopped
1 tbsp olive oil
800g (1lb 12oz) casserole lamb, cubed and tossed with 1 tbsp plain flour
2 garlic cloves, crushed
800g (1lb 12oz) waxy potatoes, such as Desiree, sliced
3 tbsp freshly chopped flat-leafed parsley
1 tsp freshly chopped thyme
300ml (½ pint) lamb stock (see page 10)
1 x 142ml carton double cream
salt and ground black pepper

1 Melt half the butter in a 3.5 litre (6¼ pint) flameproof casserole. Add the leeks and onion, stir to coat, then cover and cook over a low heat for 10 minutes.

2 Transfer the leeks and onion to a large sheet of greaseproof paper. Add the oil to the casserole and heat, then brown the meat in batches with the garlic and plenty of seasoning. Remove and put to one side on another large sheet of greaseproof paper.

3 Preheat the oven to 170°C (150°C fan oven) mark 3. Put half the potatoes in a layer over the bottom of the casserole and season with salt and pepper. Add the meat, then spoon the leek mixture on top. Arrange a layer of overlapping potatoes on top of that, sprinkle with herbs, then pour in the stock.

4 Bring the casserole to the boil, then cover and transfer to a low shelf in the oven and cook for about 1 hour 50 minutes. Remove from the oven, dot with the remaining butter and add the cream. Return to the oven and cook, uncovered, for 30–40 minutes until the potatoes are golden brown.

EASY		NUTRITIONAL INFORMATION	Serves
Preparation Time 20 minutes	**Cooking Time** 2 hours 50 minutes	**Per Serving** 530 calories, 33g fat (of which 20g saturates), 27g carbohydrate, 0.5g salt	**6**

2 tbsp olive oil

400g (14oz) lean lamb fillet, cubed

1 red onion, sliced

1 garlic clove, crushed

1 potato, peeled and quartered

1 x 400g can chopped plum tomatoes

1 red pepper, seeded and sliced

200g (7oz) canned chickpeas, drained and rinsed

1 aubergine, cut into chunks

200ml (7fl oz) lamb stock (see page 10)

1 tbsp red wine vinegar

1 tsp each freshly chopped thyme, rosemary and oregano

8 black olives, halved and pitted

salt and ground black pepper

Turkish Lamb Stew

1 Heat 1 tbsp oil in a flameproof casserole and brown the lamb over a high heat. Reduce the heat and add the remaining oil, the onion and garlic, then cook until soft.

2 Preheat the oven to 170°C (150°C fan oven) mark 3. Add the potato, tomatoes, red pepper, chickpeas, aubergine, stock, vinegar and herbs to the pan. Season, stir and bring to the boil. Cover the pan, transfer to the oven and cook for 1–1½ hours until the lamb is tender.

3 About 15 minutes before the end of the cooking time, add the olives.

Serves 4	EASY		NUTRITIONAL INFORMATION	
	Preparation Time 10 minutes	**Cooking Time** 1½ –2 hours	**Per Serving** 389 calories, 20g fat (of which 7g saturates), 28g carbohydrate, 1.2g salt	Gluten Free Dairy Free

Italian Braised Leg of Lamb

2.3kg (5lb) boned leg of lamb

50ml (2fl oz) olive oil

700g (1½lb) onions, roughly chopped

1 each red, orange and yellow peppers, seeded and roughly chopped

2 red chillies, seeded and finely chopped (see page 19)

1 garlic bulb, cloves separated and peeled

3 tbsp dried oregano

75cl bottle dry white wine

3 x 400g cans cherry tomatoes

salt and ground black pepper

1 Preheat the oven to 170°C (150°C fan oven) mark 3. Season the lamb with salt and pepper. Heat 2 tbsp oil in a large deep flameproof casserole and brown the meat well. Remove and set aside. Wipe the pan clean.

2 Heat the remaining oil in the casserole and fry the onions, peppers, chillies, garlic and oregano over a medium heat for 10–15 minutes until the onions are translucent and golden brown. Stir in the wine and tomatoes and bring to the boil. Bubble for 10 minutes.

3 Put the lamb on top of the vegetables and season. Baste the meat with the sauce and cover the casserole tightly with foil and a lid. Cook in the oven for 4 hours, basting occasionally.

4 Uncover and cook for a further 30 minutes. Serve the lamb carved into thick slices with the sauce spooned over.

EASY		NUTRITIONAL INFORMATION		Serves
Preparation Time 15 minutes	**Cooking Time** about 5 hours	**Per Serving** 400 calories, 18g fat (of which 6g saturates), 17g carbohydrate, 0.7g salt	Gluten Free Dairy Free	**6**

Pork and Apple Hotpot

1 tbsp olive oil

900g (2lb) pork shoulder steaks

3 onions, cut into wedges

1 large Bramley apple, peeled, cored and thickly sliced

1 tbsp plain flour

600ml (1 pint) hot, weak chicken or vegetable stock (see pages 10–11)

¼ savoy cabbage, sliced

2 fresh thyme sprigs

900g (2lb) large potatoes, cut into 2cm (¾in) slices

25g (1oz) butter

salt and ground black pepper

1 Preheat the oven to 170°C (150°C fan oven) mark 3. In a large non-stick flameproof casserole, heat the oil until very hot, then fry the steaks, two at a time, for 5 minutes or until golden all over. Remove the steaks from the pan and put aside.

2 In the same casserole, fry the onions for 10 minutes or until soft – add a little water if they start to stick. Stir in the apple and cook for 1 minute, then add the flour to soak up the juices. Gradually add the hot stock and stir until smooth. Season. Stir in the cabbage and add the pork.

3 Throw in the thyme, overlap the potato slices on top, then dot with the butter. Cover with a tight-fitting lid and cook near the top of the oven for 1 hour. Remove the lid and cook for 30–45 minutes until the potatoes are tender and golden.

Freezing tip

If you are going to freeze this dish, use a freezerproof casserole.

To freeze Complete the recipe, cool quickly, then freeze in the casserole for up to three months.

To use Thaw overnight at cool room temperature. Preheat the oven to 180°C (160°C fan oven) mark 4. Pour 50ml (2fl oz) hot stock over the hotpot, then cover and reheat for 30 minutes or until piping hot. Uncover and crisp the potatoes under the grill for 2–3 minutes.

Cook's Tip

Put the hotpot under the grill for 2–3 minutes to crisp up the potatoes, if you like.

Serves 4	EASY		NUTRITIONAL INFORMATION
	Preparation Time 15 minutes	**Cooking Time** 2–2¼ hours	**Per Serving** 592 calories, 18g fat (of which 7g saturates), 56g carbohydrate, 1g salt

One-pot Gammon Stew

1 tbsp olive oil

1.1kg (2½lb) smoked gammon joint

8 shallots, blanched in boiling water, drained, peeled and chopped into chunks

3 carrots, chopped into chunks

3 celery sticks, trimmed and chopped into chunks

4 large Desiree potatoes, unpeeled

450ml (¾ pint) each apple juice and hot vegetable stock (see page 10)

½ small savoy cabbage

25g (1oz) butter

1 Preheat the oven to 190°C (170°C fan oven) mark 5. Heat the oil in a large flameproof casserole. Add the gammon and brown all over. Remove from the pan.

2 Add the shallots, carrots and celery to the pan and fry for 10 minutes over a low heat until starting to soften.

3 Return the gammon to the pan. Chop the potatoes into quarters and add to the pan with the apple juice and hot stock. Cover and bring to the boil, then transfer to the oven and cook for 50 minutes or until the meat is cooked through and the vegetables are tender.

4 Remove from the oven and put the dish back on the hob over a low heat. Shred the cabbage and stir into the pan. Simmer for 2–3 minutes, then stir in the butter and serve.

EASY		NUTRITIONAL INFORMATION		Serves
Preparation Time 15 minutes	**Cooking Time** 1 hour 20 minutes	**Per Serving** 680 calories, 30g fat (of which 11g saturates), 41g carbohydrate, 6.3g salt	Gluten Free	**4**

Cook's Tip

The sweetness of buttered parsnips makes them an ideal accompaniment to pork. Cut about 700g (1½lb) scrubbed, unpeeled parsnips into chunky lengths from the stalk to the root end. Melt 50g (2oz) butter in a deep frying pan and add the parsnips. Stir over the heat for 5–7 minutes, shaking the pan occasionally, until the parsnips are tender and have a wonderful sticky glaze.

Roast Pork Loin with Rosemary and Mustard

2 tbsp freshly chopped rosemary

4 tbsp Dijon mustard

50ml (2fl oz) lemon juice

50g (2oz) light muscovado sugar

175g (6oz) honey

1 tbsp soy sauce

1.4kg (3lb) loin of pork, chine bone (backbone) removed, rib bones cut off and separated into individual ribs (ask the butcher to do this for you)

lemon wedges and rosemary sprigs to serve

1 Preheat the oven to 200°C (180°C) mark 6. Mix together the rosemary, mustard, lemon juice, sugar, honey and soy sauce and put to one side.

2 Put the loin into a roasting tin and cook in the oven for 40 minutes.

3 Add the ribs to the roasting tin and cook the pork for a further 40 minutes.

4 Drain off any fat and brush the pork with the mustard glaze. Put back in the oven for about 15 minutes, basting occasionally with the glaze or until well browned and tender. Serve hot or cold, garnished with rosemary and lemon.

Serves 8	EASY		NUTRITIONAL INFORMATION	
	Preparation Time 5 minutes	**Cooking Time** 1 hour 35 minutes	**Per Serving** 354 calories, 13g fat (of which 4g saturates), 24g carbohydrate, 1.1g salt	Dairy Free

Try Something Different

Instead of pork, use the same quantity of lean lamb, such as leg, trimmed of excess fat and cut into cubes.

Without a Slow Cooker

Follow the recipe until the end of step 2, but fry the pork in a flameproof casserole. In step 2, bring to the boil, then transfer to the oven and cook for 25 minutes. Complete the recipe from step 3.

Spicy Pork and Bean Stew

3 tbsp olive oil

400g (14oz) pork tenderloin, cubed

1 red onion, sliced

2 leeks, trimmed and cut into chunks

2 celery sticks, trimmed and cut into chunks

½ tbsp harissa paste

1 tbsp tomato purée

1 x 400g can cherry tomatoes

150ml (5fl oz) hot vegetable or chicken stock (see pages 10–11)

salt and ground black pepper

1 x 400g can cannellini beans, drained and rinsed

1 marinated red pepper, sliced

freshly chopped flat-leafed parsley

Greek-style yogurt, lemon wedges and bread, to serve

1 Heat 2 tbsp olive oil in a large pan and fry the pork in batches until golden. Transfer to the slow cooker.

2 Heat the remaining oil in the pan and fry the onion for 5–10 minutes until softened. Add the leek and celery and cook for 5 minutes. Add the harissa and tomato purée. Cook for 1–2 minutes, stirring all the time. Add the tomatoes and stock and season well. Bring to the boil, then pour into the slow cooker. Cover and cook for 3–4 hours on Low.

3 Stir in the drained beans and red pepper and leave to stand for 5 minutes to warm through. Garnish with parsley and serve with a dollop of Greek yogurt, a grinding of black pepper, lemon wedges for squeezing over the stew, and chunks of crusty baguette or wholegrain bread.

EASY		NUTRITIONAL INFORMATION		Serves
Preparation Time 15 minutes	**Cooking Time** 3–4 hours on Low	**Per Serving** 348 calories, 14g fat (of which 3g saturates), 27g carbohydrate, 1.5g salt	Gluten Free	**4**

Pheasant Casserole with Cider and Apples

2 large, oven-ready pheasants
2 tbsp plain flour, plus extra to dust
50g (2oz) butter
4 rindless streaky bacon rashers, halved
2 onions, chopped
2 celery sticks, trimmed and chopped
1 tbsp dried juniper berries, lightly crushed
2.5cm (1in) piece fresh root ginger, peeled and finely chopped
150ml (¼ pint) hot pheasant or chicken stock (see page 10)
350ml (12fl oz) dry cider
150ml (¼ pint) double cream
4 crisp eating apples, such as Granny Smith
1 tbsp lemon juice
salt and ground black pepper

1 Cut each pheasant into four portions, season with salt and pepper and dust with flour.

2 Melt three-quarters of the butter in a large pan and brown the pheasant portions, in batches, over a high heat until deep golden brown on all sides. Transfer to the slow cooker.

3 Add the bacon to the pan and fry for 2–3 minutes until golden. Add the onions, celery, juniper and ginger and cook for 8–10 minutes.

4 Stir in the flour and cook, stirring, for 2 minutes, then add the hot stock and the cider and bring to the boil, stirring. Pour into the slow cooker and season well, then cover and cook on Low for 6–7 hours or until the pheasant is tender.

5 Lift out the pheasant and put into a warmed dish and keep it warm. Strain the sauce through a sieve into a pan. Stir in the cream, bring to the boil and bubble for 10 minutes or until syrupy.

6 Quarter, core and cut the apples into wedges, then toss in the lemon juice. Melt the remaining butter in a small pan and fry the apple wedges for 2–3 minutes until golden. Return the pheasant to the sauce, along with the apples, and check the seasoning before serving.

EASY		NUTRITIONAL INFORMATION	Serves
Preparation Time 50 minutes	**Cooking Time** 40 minutes in pan and 6–7 hours on Low	**Per Serving** 478 calories, 28g fat (of which 16g saturates), 12g carbohydrate, 0.7g salt	8

Rabbit Casserole with Prunes

175g (6oz) ready-to-eat pitted prunes

300ml (½ pint) red wine

3–4 tbsp olive oil

about 2.3kg (5lb) rabbit joints

1 large onion, chopped

2 large garlic cloves, crushed

5 tbsp Armagnac

450ml (¾ pint) light chicken or vegetable stock (see pages 10–11)

a few fresh thyme sprigs, tied together, or 1 tsp dried thyme, plus extra sprigs to garnish

2 bay leaves

150ml (¼ pint) double cream

125g (4oz) brown-cap mushrooms, sliced

salt and ground black pepper

1 Put the prunes and wine into a bowl. Cover and leave for about 4 hours, then strain, keeping the wine and prunes to one side.

2 Preheat the oven to 170°C (150°C fan oven) mark 3. Heat 3 tbsp oil in a flameproof casserole. Brown the rabbit joints a few at a time, then remove from the casserole. Add the onion and garlic with a little more oil, if needed, and brown lightly. Put the rabbit back into the casserole, add the Armagnac and warm through. Carefully light the Armagnac with a taper or long match, then shake the pan gently until the flames subside.

3 Pour in the stock and the wine from the prunes and bring to the boil. Add the thyme sprigs or dried thyme to the casserole with the bay leaves and plenty of salt and pepper. Cover tightly and cook in the oven for about 1 hour or until tender.

4 Lift the rabbit out of the juices and keep warm. Boil the cooking juices until reduced by half. Add the cream and mushrooms and continue boiling for 2–3 minutes. Stir in the prunes and warm through. Adjust the seasoning, then spoon the sauce over the rabbit to serve. Garnish with sprigs of fresh thyme.

Serves	EASY		NUTRITIONAL INFORMATION	
6	**Preparation Time** 20 minutes, plus soaking	**Cooking Time** 1 hour 35 minutes	**Per Serving** 538 calories, 26g fat (of which 13g saturates), 11g carbohydrate, 0.5g salt	Gluten Free

4

Vegetarian

Without a Slow Cooker

Complete the recipe to the end of step 2, but leaving out the beans. Cover the pan and simmer for 20 minutes or until the vegetables are tender. Add the beans and cook for 3 minutes to warm through. Serve immediately.

Try Something Different

Instead of paprika, use 1 tsp each ground cumin and ground coriander. Garnish with freshly chopped coriander.

Spiced Bean and Vegetable Stew

3 tbsp olive oil

2 small onions, sliced

2 garlic cloves, crushed

1 tbsp sweet paprika

1 small dried red chilli, seeded and finely chopped

700g (1½lb) sweet potatoes, cubed

700g (1½lb) pumpkin, cut into chunks

125g (4oz) okra, trimmed

500g passata (See Cook's Tip on page 41)

400g can haricot or cannellini beans, drained and rinsed

450ml (¾ pint) hot vegetable stock

salt and ground black pepper

1 Heat the oil in a large pan over a very gentle heat. Add the onions and garlic and cook for 5 minutes.

2 Stir in the paprika and chilli and cook for 2 minutes, then add the sweet potatoes, pumpkin, okra, passata, beans and hot stock. Season generously with salt and pepper and bring to the boil.

3 Transfer to the slow cooker, cover and cook on Low for 2–3 hours until the vegetables are tender.

Serves 6	EASY		NUTRITIONAL INFORMATION	
	Preparation Time 15 minutes	**Cooking Time** 10 minutes in pan then 2–3 hours on Low	**Per Serving** 262 calories, 7g fat (of which 1g saturates), 44g carbohydrate, 1.3g salt	Vegetarian Gluten Free • Dairy Free

Without a Slow Cooker

At the end of step 2, leave the mixture in the pan, half cover with a lid, and simmer over a low heat for 25–30 minutes. Complete the recipe from step 3.

Lentils with Red Pepper

1 tbsp olive oil

1 large onion, finely chopped

2 celery sticks, trimmed and diced

2 carrots, diced

2 bay leaves, torn

300g (11oz) Puy lentils

600ml (1 pint) hot vegetable stock (see page 10)

1 marinated red pepper, drained and chopped

2 tbsp chopped flat-leafed parsley, plus extra to garnish

ground black pepper

1 Heat the oil in a pan, add the onion and cook over a low heat for 15 minutes or until soft. Add the celery, carrots and bay leaves and cook for 2 minutes.

2 Add the lentils with the hot stock and stir everything together. Transfer to the slow cooker, cover and cook on High for 3–4 hours.

3 Stir in the red pepper and parsley and season with pepper. Leave to stand for 10 minutes, then garnish with extra parsley and serve as an accompaniment.

EASY		NUTRITIONAL INFORMATION		Serves
Preparation Time 10 minutes	**Cooking Time** 20 minutes in pan then 3–4 hours on High	**Per Serving** 296 calories, 5g fat (of which 1g saturates), 47g carbohydrate, 0.1g salt	Vegetarian Gluten Free • Dairy Free	**4**

Without a Slow Cooker

Grease a 1.7 litre (3 pint) ovenproof dish instead of the slow cooker. Cover with foil and cook in the oven for 1 hour until soft.

Braised Chicory in White Wine

50g (2oz) butter, softened
juice of ½ lemon
6 heads of chicory, trimmed
salt and ground black pepper
100ml (3½fl oz) white wine
snipped chives to serve

1 Grease the slow cooker dish with 15g (½oz) butter. Toss the chicory in the lemon juice and lay in the base.

2 Season to taste, add the wine and dot the remaining butter over the top. Cover and cook on Low for 2–3 hours until soft. Scatter with chives to serve.

Serves 4	EASY		NUTRITIONAL INFORMATION	
	Preparation Time 5 minutes	**Cooking Time** 2–3 hours on Low	**Per Serving** 80 calories, 7g fat (of which 5g saturates), 3g carbohydrate, 0.1g salt	Gluten Free Vegetarian

Without a Slow Cooker

Heat 2 tbsp olive oil in a large heavy-based pan, add the onion and cook gently for 3–4 minutes to soften. Add the cabbage, sugar, spices, vinegars and orange juice, and season well. Bring to the boil, lower the heat, then cover the pan and simmer for 30 minutes. Add the apples and stir through. Cook for a further 15 minutes or until the cabbage is tender and nearly all the liquid has evaporated. Discard the cinnamon stick before serving.

½ medium red cabbage, about 500g (1lb 2oz), shredded

1 red onion, finely chopped

1 Bramley apple, peeled, cored and chopped

25g (1oz) light muscovado sugar

1 cinnamon stick

pinch of ground cloves

¼ tsp freshly grated nutmeg

2 tbsp each red wine vinegar and red wine

juice of 1 orange

salt and ground black pepper

Braised Red Cabbage

1 Put all the ingredients into the slow cooker and stir to mix well. Cover and cook on Low for 2–3 hours.

2 When the cabbage is tender, remove the pan from the heat and discard the cinnamon stick. Serve at once, or cool, put into a bowl, cover and chill the cabbage overnight.

3 To reheat, put the cabbage into a pan, add 2 tbsp cold water and cover with a tight-fitting lid. Bring to the boil, then reduce the heat and simmer for 25 minutes.

EASY		NUTRITIONAL INFORMATION		Serves
Preparation Time 10 minutes	**Cooking Time** 2–3 hours on Low	**Per Serving** 50 calories, trace fat, 11g carbohydrate, 0g salt	Vegetarian Gluten Free • Dairy Free	**8**

Ratatouille

4 tbsp olive oil

2 onions, thinly sliced

1 large garlic clove, crushed

350g (12oz) small aubergines, thinly sliced

450g (1lb) small courgettes, thinly sliced

450g (1lb) tomatoes, skinned, seeded and roughly chopped

1 green and 1 red pepper, each cored, seeded and sliced

1 tbsp chopped basil

2 tsp freshly chopped thyme

2 tbsp freshly chopped flat-leafed parsley

2 tbsp sun-dried tomato paste

salt and ground black pepper

1 Heat the oil in a large pan, add the onions and garlic and fry gently for 10 minutes or until softened and golden.

2 Add the aubergines, courgettes, tomatoes, sliced peppers, herbs, tomato paste and seasoning. Fry, stirring, for 2–3 minutes.

3 Transfer to the slow cooker and cover. Cook on High for 3–4 hours until all the vegetables are tender. Taste and adjust the seasoning. Serve the ratatouille hot or at room temperature.

Without a Slow Cooker

At the start of step 3, leave the mixture in the pan, cover tightly and simmer for 30 minutes or until all the vegetables are tender. Uncover towards the end if there is too much liquid. Season and serve as described in step 3.

Serves	EASY		NUTRITIONAL INFORMATION	
6	**Preparation Time** 20 minutes	**Cooking Time** 15 minutes in pan then 3–4 hours on High	**Per Serving** 150 calories, 9g fat (of which 1g saturates), 15g carbohydrate, 0.1g salt	Vegetarian Gluten Free • Dairy Free

Cook's Tip

This is an ideal accompaniment to grilled fish or meat, or a
vegetarian frittata.

Baked Tomatoes and Fennel

900g (2lb) fennel, trimmed and cut into quarters
75ml (2½fl oz) white wine
5 thyme sprigs
75ml (2½fl oz) olive oil
900g (2lb) ripe beef or plum tomatoes

1 Preheat the oven to 200°C (180°C fan oven) mark 6.
Put the fennel into a roasting tin and pour the wine
over it. Snip the thyme sprigs over the fennel, drizzle
with the oil and roast for 45 minutes.

2 Halve the tomatoes, add to the roasting tin and
continue to roast for 30 minutes or until tender,
basting with the juices halfway through.

Serves	EASY		NUTRITIONAL INFORMATION	
6	**Preparation Time** 10 minutes	**Cooking Time** 1¼ hours	**Per Serving** 127 calories, 9g fat (of which 1g saturates), 7g carbohydrate, 0.1g salt	Vegetarian Gluten Free • Dairy Free

5

Puddings

Baked Rice Pudding

butter to grease

125g (4oz) short-grain pudding rice

1.1 litres (2 pints) full-fat milk

50g (2oz) golden caster sugar

1 tsp vanilla extract

grated zest of 1 orange (optional)

freshly grated nutmeg to taste

1 Preheat the oven to 170°C (150°C fan oven) mark 3. Lightly butter a 1.7 litre (3 pint) ovenproof dish. Add the rice, milk, sugar, vanilla extract and orange zest, if using, and stir everything together. Grate the nutmeg over the top of the mixture.

2 Bake the pudding in the middle of the oven for 1½ hours or until the top is golden brown.

Serves	EASY		NUTRITIONAL INFORMATION	
6	**Preparation Time** 5 minutes	**Cooking Time** 1½ hours	**Per Serving** 239 calories, 8g fat (of which 5g saturates), 34g carbohydrate, 0.2g salt	Vegetarian Gluten Free

Try Something Different

For an alternative presentation, serve in tumblers, layering the rice pudding with the fruit sauce; you will need to use double the amount of fruit sauce.

Without a Slow Cooker

Put the rice into a pan with 600ml (1 pint) cold water. Bring to the boil, then reduce the heat and simmer until the liquid has evaporated. Add the milk, bring to the boil, then reduce the heat and simmer for 45 minutes until soft and creamy. Leave to cool, then complete the recipe from step 2.

Fruity Rice Pudding

125g (4oz) short-grain pudding rice
1.1 litres (2 pints) full-fat milk
1 tsp vanilla extract
3–4 tbsp caster sugar
200ml (7fl oz) whipping cream
6 tbsp wild lingonberry sauce

1 Put the rice into the slow cooker with the milk, vanilla extract and sugar. Cover and cook on Low for 2–3 hours. You can enjoy the pudding hot now or leave to cool and continue the recipe.

2 Lightly whip the cream and fold through the pudding. Chill for 1 hour.

3 Divide the rice mixture among six glass dishes and top with 1 tbsp lingonberry sauce.

EASY		NUTRITIONAL INFORMATION		Serves
Preparation Time 10 minutes, plus cooling and chilling (optional)	**Cooking Time** 2–3 hours on Low	**Per Serving** 323 calories, 17g fat (of which 10g saturates), 36g carbohydrate, 0.2g salt	Vegetarian Gluten Free	**6**

Cook's Tip

Brandy Butter
Put 125g (4oz) unsalted butter in a bowl and beat until very soft. Gradually beat in 125g (4oz) sieved light muscovado sugar until very light and fluffy, then beat in 6 tbsp brandy, a spoonful at a time. Cover and chill for at least 3 hours.

Cranberry Christmas Pudding

200g (7oz) currants
200g (7oz) sultanas
200g (7oz) raisins
75g (3oz) dried cranberries or cherries
grated zest and juice of 1 orange
50ml (2fl oz) rum
50ml (2fl oz) brandy
1–2 tsp Angostura bitters
1 small apple, peeled and grated
1 carrot, grated
175g (6oz) fresh breadcrumbs
100g (3½oz) plain flour, sifted
1 tsp mixed spice
175g (6oz) light vegetarian suet
100g (3½oz) dark muscovado sugar
50g (2oz) blanched almonds, roughly chopped
2 medium eggs
butter to grease
fresh or frozen cranberries (thawed if frozen), fresh bay leaves and icing sugar to decorate
Brandy Butter (see Cook's Tip) to serve

1 Put the dried fruit, orange zest and juice into a large bowl. Pour the rum, brandy and Angostura bitters over. Cover and leave to soak in a cool place for at least 1 hour or overnight.

2 Add the apple, carrot, breadcrumbs, flour, mixed spice, suet, sugar, almonds and eggs to the bowl of soaked fruit. Use a wooden spoon to mix everything together well. Grease a 1.8 litre (3¼ pint) pudding basin and line with a 60cm (24in) square piece of muslin. Spoon the mixture into the basin and flatten the surface. Gather the muslin up and over the top, twist and secure with string. Put the basin on an upturned heatproof saucer or trivet in the base of a large pan, then pour in enough boiling water to come halfway up the side of the basin. Cover with a tight-fitting lid and simmer for 6 hours. Keep the water topped up with more boiling water.

3 Remove the basin from the pan and leave to cool. When the pudding is cold, remove from the basin, then wrap it in clingfilm and a double layer of foil. Store in a cool, dry place for up to six months.

4 To reheat, steam for 2½ hours; check the water level every 40 minutes and top up if necessary. Leave the pudding in the pan, covered, to keep warm until needed. Decorate with cranberries and bay leaves, dust with icing sugar and serve with Brandy Butter.

EASY		NUTRITIONAL INFORMATION		Serves
Preparation Time 20 minutes, plus soaking	**Cooking Time** 8½ hours	**Per Serving** 448 calories, 17g fat (of which 7g saturates), 68g carbohydrate, 0.3g salt	Vegetarian	**12**

Orange and Chocolate Cheesecake

225g (8oz) chilled unsalted butter, plus extra to grease

250g (9oz) plain flour, sifted

150g (5oz) light muscovado sugar

3 tbsp cocoa powder

chocolate curls to decorate (see page 283, optional)

For the topping

2 oranges

800g (1lb 12oz) cream cheese

250g (9oz) mascarpone cheese

4 large eggs

225g (8oz) golden caster sugar

2 tbsp cornflour

½ tsp vanilla extract

1 vanilla pod

1 Preheat the oven to 180°C (160°C fan oven) mark 4. Grease a 23cm (9in) springform cake tin and base-line with baking parchment.

2 Cut 175g (6oz) butter into cubes. Melt the remaining butter and set aside. Put the flour and cubed butter into a food processor with the sugar and cocoa powder. Whiz until the texture of fine breadcrumbs. (Alternatively, rub the butter into the flour in a large bowl by hand or using a pastry blender. Stir in the sugar and cocoa.) Pour in the melted butter and pulse, or stir with a fork, until the mixture comes together.

3 Spoon the crumb mixture into the prepared tin and press evenly on to the base, using the back of a metal spoon to level the surface. Bake for 35–40 minutes until lightly puffed; avoid over-browning or the biscuit base will have a bitter flavour. Remove from the oven and allow to cool. Reduce the oven temperature to 150°C (130°C fan oven) mark 2.

4 Meanwhile, make the topping. Grate the zest from the oranges, then squeeze the juice – you will need 150ml (¼ pint). Put the cream cheese, mascarpone, eggs, sugar, cornflour, grated orange zest and vanilla extract into a large bowl. Using a hand-held electric whisk, beat the ingredients together thoroughly until well combined.

5 Split the vanilla pod in half lengthways and, using the tip of a sharp knife, scrape out the seeds and add them to the cheese mixture. Beat in the orange juice and continue whisking until the mixture is smooth.

6 Pour the cheese mixture over the cooled biscuit base. Bake for about 1½ hours or until pale golden on top, slightly risen and just set around the edge. The cheesecake should still be slightly wobbly in the middle; it will set as it cools. Turn off the oven and leave the cheesecake inside, with the door ajar, to cool for 1 hour. Remove and allow to cool completely (about 3 hours), then chill.

7 Just before serving, unclip the tin and transfer the cheesecake to a plate. Scatter chocolate curls on top to decorate, if you like.

Serves 4	EASY		NUTRITIONAL INFORMATION
	Preparation Time 45 minutes	**Cooking Time** 2–2¼ hours, plus cooling	**Per Serving** 767 calories, 60g fat (of which 37g saturates), 53g carbohydrate, 1.2g salt

Try Something Different

Instead of syrup, try the following:
Steamed Jam Sponge Puddings
Put 4 tbsp raspberry or blackberry jam into the bottom
of the basins instead of the syrup.
Steamed Chocolate Sponge Puddings
Omit the golden syrup. Blend 4 tbsp cocoa powder with
2 tbsp hot water, then gradually beat into the creamed
mixture before adding the eggs.

Steamed Syrup Sponge Puddings

125g (4oz) unsalted butter, softened, plus extra to grease

3 tbsp golden syrup

125g (4oz) golden caster sugar

few drops of vanilla extract

2 medium eggs, beaten

175g (6oz) self-raising flour, sifted

about 3 tbsp milk

custard or cream to serve

1 Half-fill a steamer or large pan with water and put it on to boil. Grease four 300ml (½ pint) basins or a 900ml (1½ pint) pudding basin and spoon the golden syrup into the bottom of the basin(s).

2 Cream the butter and sugar together in a bowl until pale and fluffy. Stir in the vanilla extract. Add the eggs, a little at a time, beating well after each addition.

3 Using a metal spoon, fold in half the flour, then fold in the remaining flour with enough milk to give a dropping consistency. Spoon the mixture into the prepared pudding basin(s).

4 Cover with greased and pleated greaseproof paper and foil, and secure with string. Steam for 35 minutes for individual puddings or 1½ hours for one large pudding, checking the water level from time to time and topping up with boiling water as necessary. Turn out on to warmed plates and serve with custard or cream.

Serves 4	EASY		NUTRITIONAL INFORMATION	
	Preparation Time 20 minutes	**Cooking Time** 35 minutes or 1½ hours	**Per Serving** 580 calories, 29g fat (of which 17g saturates), 76g carbohydrate, 0.7g salt	Vegetarian

To Store

Store in an airtight container. It will keep for up to one week.

Raspberry and Peach Cake

200g (7oz) unsalted butter, melted, plus extra to grease

250g (9oz) self-raising flour, sifted

100g (3½oz) golden caster sugar

4 medium eggs, beaten

125g (4oz) raspberries

2 large, almost-ripe peaches or nectarines, halved, stoned and sliced

4 tbsp apricot jam

juice of ½ lemon

1 Preheat the oven to 190°C (170°C fan oven) mark 5. Grease a 20.5cm (8in) springform cake tin and base-line with baking parchment.

2 Put the flour and sugar into a large bowl. Make a well in the centre and add the melted butter and the eggs. Mix well.

3 Spread half the mixture over the base of the cake tin and add half the raspberries and sliced peaches or nectarines. Spoon on the remaining cake mixture, smooth over, then add the remaining raspberries and peaches or nectarines, pressing them down into the mixture slightly.

4 Bake for 1–1¼ hours until risen and golden and a skewer inserted into the centre comes out clean. Remove from the oven and leave in the tin to cool for 10 minutes.

5 Warm the jam and the lemon juice together in a small pan and brush over the cake to glaze. Serve warm or at room temperature.

EASY		NUTRITIONAL INFORMATION		Serves
Preparation Time 15 minutes	**Cooking Time** 1 1¼ hours, plus cooling	**Per Serving** 405 calories, 24g fat (of which 14g saturates), 44g carbohydrate, 0.8g salt	Vegetarian	**8**

Try Something Different

Replace the figs with dried apple rings and the pears with raisins.

Without a Slow Cooker

Put the dried fruits, spices, apple juice and wine in a pan and bring to the boil slowly. Reduce the heat, cover and simmer for 45 minutes until the fruits are plump and tender. Top up the liquid if necessary. Complete the recipe from step 3.

Winter Fruit Compote

75g (3oz) ready-to-eat dried pears

75g (3oz) ready-to-eat dried figs

75g (3oz) ready-to-eat dried apricots

75g (3oz) ready-to-eat prunes

1 star anise

½ cinnamon stick

300ml (½ pint) apple juice

300ml (½ pint) dry white wine

light muscovado sugar to taste

crème fraîche or thick Greek-style yogurt to serve

1 Put the dried fruits into the slow cooker with the star anise and cinnamon stick.

2 Put the apple juice and wine into a pan and bring to the boil. Pour over the fruit, cover and cook on Low for 3–4 hours until plump and tender.

3 Turn the compote out into a bowl. Taste the cooking liquid for sweetness, adding a little sugar if necessary. Leave to cool to room temperature.

4 Serve the compote with crème fraîche or thick Greek-style yogurt.

Serves 6	EASY		NUTRITIONAL INFORMATION	
	Preparation Time 10 minutes	**Cooking Time** 5 minutes in pan then 3–4 hours on Low	**Per Serving** 139 calories, trace fat, 26g carbohydrate, 0.1g salt	Vegetarian Gluten Free